GOD'S DREAM

Our greatest privilege

Mark and Fiona Gilpin

Evangelism Reimagined

Evangelism Reimagined
www.evangelismreimagined.org
ISBN 978-1-909996-15-1

A Catalogue record for this book is available from the British Library.

Produced by Evangelism Reimagined Publishing
info@evangelismreimagined.org
Printed and bound in Great Britain

Strong's Definitions are referenced from www.blueletterbible.org.

These are a collection of the unique Greek and Hebrew words and their definitions from
the Old and New Testament, organized by Dr James Strong in 1890.

The names and details of people in our stories have been changed to protect their anonymity.

ABOUT THE AUTHORS

Mark and Fiona help lead the growth of an evangelistic culture at Eastgate Church[1] in North Kent, introducing people to the joy of partnering with God in evangelism. Mark helps people to discover a motivation for evangelism and shows them how they have been designed to be evangelistic. Fiona helps people find freedom from negative experiences of evangelism and to embrace the adventure that evangelism is meant to be.

They are both passionate about enabling others to enjoy speaking about Jesus confidently and courageously. They create an approach to evangelism that is fun, adventurous, and accessible to all believers without guilt, shame, or condemnation.

They both love to bring the reality of the Kingdom of God to unbelievers wherever they are. They bring a confidence to supernatural evangelism, and a way of introducing people to Jesus that creates a desire for more.

Mark and Fiona are authors of the Developing a Supernatural Evangelistic Lifestyle[2] (DASEL) training course, which helps churches and individuals to reimagine evangelism from God's perspective and develop an evangelistic culture and lifestyle.

---

[1] eastgate.org.uk
[2] www.dasel.info

We dedicate this book to Phyllis Gilpin. Your untimely death has left an unfillable gap in our family. Some of our children never had the opportunity and privilege to meet you.

Thank you for being an amazing mother, mother-in-law, and nana. Your example to us of what an evangelist is has shaped and helped us on our journey to reimagine evangelism. We miss you.

To be a soul winner is the happiest thing in the world.
And with every soul you bring to Jesus Christ, you seem
to get a new heaven here upon earth.

Charles Spurgeon
(Baptist Pastor and Author, 19th century)

VIII

CONTENTS

FOREWORD

Imagine that, God is a dreamer!

God has a very active imagination and he dreamed of creating the earth and then placing on it human beings made in his image with whom he would have intimate friendship; these humans would have the privilege and responsibility of ruling over the earth in a godly way to create "heaven on earth".

The book of Ephesians tells us that it was for His pleasure that God created the earth; God's dream is for humans to live in loving relationship with Him and through this relationship understand how to create Heaven's environment on earth. That was the purpose of creation.

Fundamental to that dream is the concept of freedom: human beings free to make choices and take responsibility, rather than slaves who simply have to obey the instructions of a cosmic dictator.

In the Garden of Eden freedom to choose was given by God to humanity; a bad choice was made and the subsequent consequence was that humans were separated from their intimate relationship with God, and instead of creating heaven on earth humans allowed evil to be brought into the world.

It is not difficult to see evil in our world: hatred, war, violence, and greed are examples, and the consequences of such things lead to all sorts of distress and disorder.

However, God does not change, He is still a dreamer. And here is the dream: to draw mankind back into intimate relationship with Him, Father God reconnected with His children, and from there heaven on earth to be reclaimed and restored.

In this book, Mark and Fiona are redefining the concept of evangelism and putting it back into the context outlined above. Evangelism is about joining in with God's dream for mankind and the earth and as it unfolds, we get to share in the pleasure of God, the Father, Son and Holy Spirit. This concept has had a dramatic impact upon Eastgate, the church of which I am a part.

Evangelism is no longer viewed as an obligation that we must endeavour to do, no matter how reluctant we may feel, it is viewed as joining in with the pleasure of God. We proclaim the good news of Jesus Christ and His kingdom. And indeed it is good news accompanied by signs, wonders and miracles as God confirms his message of grace and eternal life in relationship with Him.

This book is not just theory, it is backed up by the very lives that flow through its pages, with countless great, heart-warming stories. It contains very practical teaching and instruction; it is very approachable. I have witnessed the fruit of this personally and my life has been enriched.

This book could change your life! And not just yours.

Imagine this: introducing people to Jesus will bear fruit that will last for all eternity, for God's dream doesn't just cover this temporary earthly reality but beyond that pulls people through His love and power into an eternal reality of living in Heaven.

That is quite a dream.

Dr Pete Carter
Director of Eastgate, founder of Heaven in Healthcare and author of Unwrapping Lazarus.

GOD'S DREAM

PREFACE

*The system is not working. That is how a
paradigm shift begins:
the established way of seeing the world no
longer functions.*
(Matthew Fox, Actor)

We have both been Christians for over thirty years and have seen
and experienced many different approaches to evangelism. Even
though we have seen many people come to Christ, it has left us
with unanswered questions. The two that stand out are: why within
modern western culture do we see relatively fewer people saved and
why do so many Christians struggle with evangelism?

Our heart's desire has long been to seek the most authentic, loving,
and Biblical approach to introduce Jesus to people who do not yet
know him. We want people to discover who he really is, and what
he is really like so that they can truly believe in him and give their
all to follow him.

This book tells our own story about evangelism and the answers
we are finding to our questions. Seeing Jesus as the evangelist and
how he introduces his kingdom to unbelievers has led us to rethink
evangelism. We introduce paradigms about evangelism that will be

familiar to some, but will be new to many.

These paradigms challenge some long-standing perspectives, approaches, and traditional practices about evangelism. We don't do this lightly or with disrespect. Do we need to look afresh at evangelism from a Biblical perspective, rather than continuing with our current experience? Is it possible to see all Christians engage in the Great Commission, without reimagining evangelism from God's perspective?

Our deepest hope is to see all Christians equipped to freely enjoy sharing their faith as a lifestyle. To achieve this, we believe it requires introducing some different paradigms about evangelism. If Jesus is our prime example of how to do evangelism, what can we learn from him?

"For God so loved the world that he gave his one and only Son, that whoever believes in him shall not perish but have eternal life. For God did not send his Son into the world to condemn the world, but to save the world through him" (John 3:16-17).

ACKNOWLEDGEMENTS

We would like to thank the Directors at Eastgate Church for your encouragement in this venture and the amount of trust, freedom, and opportunities you have given us. We particularly want to thank Pete Carter, Kim Carter, David Webster and Vicky Schulz for believing in us and helping us see the significance of the God's Dream and Evangelism Freedom messages.

We also want to thank the evangelists at Eastgate Church and the students at Eastgate School of Spiritual Life (ESSL) for partnering with us as we reimagined evangelism. Your friendship, support, and encouragement have helped us go further.

Thank you to our friends who have supported and encouraged us in the writing of this book. Your friendship, time, and feedback have been invaluable.

GOD'S DREAM

ENDORSEMENTS

Mark and Fiona are the real deal, evangelists who love encouraging and equipping people to share God's love. Here, in *God's Dream* they demonstrate how they have helped transform Eastgate's perspective on and practice of evangelism. Their infectious joy and love for others shines through in this book.

Travelling with them is always a great experience, Mark and Fiona truly do create a 'slipstream' for others to flow in their Holy Spirit created evangelistic DNA. I have witnessed both their lives at first hand, and love their passion for God and people. For many, *God's Dream* will redeem the concept and practice of evangelism. It is practical and theologically thorough.

A wider distribution of Kingdom theology and empowered practice contained in these pages, will not only lead to happier evangelistic people but the advance of Jesus' love and power in our nation. As you read *God's Dream* you will be inspired to move in the supernatural, release the Kingdom of God, and partner with him to reconcile the world to himself.

David Webster
Eastgate Church Director and author of Your Royal Identity

Mark and Fiona are a powerful combination. They bring wisdom, experience, infectious enthusiasm, challenge, gentleness, compassion, love, and of course, boundless energy and passion for Jesus! Their creative thinking, and their message that every believer is wired to share the goodness of God with those around them, will inspire and empower you to live out your own unique evangelistic shape.

I have, over many years, seen them take hundreds of students by the hand and lead them into the joy of discovering how to share the good news of the Kingdom in our local community. They are natural evangelists and this book will nudge you in to an exciting new way of discovering God's heart for reaching others. This is going to be fun!

Vicky Schulz
Head of Eastgate Day School of Spiritual Life

Talk to most British Christians about their least favourite church activity and the chances are Evangelism will be up there at the top of the list. The truth is many of us have had bad experiences, been taught wrong motives, picked up dodgy methodology and have misunderstood the Father's heart. This book is a real tonic for all of us who feel out of our depth with the big 'E'.

Laced with brilliant real life stories and examples of how easy evangelism can be when we partner with the Holy Spirit; Mark and Fiona's book gently addresses the places our thinking and experiences can be out of sync with the King and His Kingdom. Page by page they lead you to a place where evangelism can be fear free, fun and fruitful. Go on give it a read, step out of your comfort zone and enter the place where the miracle of new life happens!

Mark Hendley
Director of The Stones Cry Out and Head of Eastgate Evening School of Spiritual Life

This is the best book I have read on evangelism in the past ten years. Very accessible, extremely practical, with lots of illustrations; it exudes evangelism as a great adventure.

It is also a groundbreaking book. Why? Because up until now evangelism in the West has often focussed on cut down versions of the Gospel that either focus on just sin, repentance, forgiveness and then going to heaven or on just healing and the power of God. This book rightly brings us back to the full Gospel, which is preaching Jesus and the Kingdom, and demonstrating it with power, as something we are all called to do.

Derrick Burns
YWAM Missionary

When you meet Mark and Fiona Gilpin, you meet two people who really love God and they allow that love to flow through them, to the person in front of them, whether that is you, someone in your church or a person who doesn't know Jesus. They are also people who model prophecy, healing, and other gifts of the Spirit as being normal parts of the Christian life. It is therefore not a surprise that this teaching on evangelism is powered by Holy Spirit and motivated by love.

"Evangelism" is a word that brings many Christians, and even pastors like us, out in a nervous sweat! However, we found that the Developing a Supernatural Evangelistic Lifestyle (DASEL) course format of talks, inspiring stories, discussion, and practical "activations" were the perfect way to grow together as a church in evangelism.

Their material is incredibly freeing because it doesn't teach programme or structure, but instead teaches connection and identity. It shows how we can join in with what God is already doing. As a church we saw that evangelism can be fun, easy and something for every generation. It brought great freedom and even relief that we don't have to become someone else in order to share about Jesus. God wants to use us as we are.

We would recommend DASEL and even getting a visit from Mark and Fiona to help you personally, and as a church, to grow in this beautiful gift – sharing the love of God with those around you.

Adrian and Esther Jervis
Pastors of Åkerbo Frikyrkoförsamling (Åkerbo Free Church)
Linköping, Sweden

We hosted a Developing a Supernatural Evangelistic Lifestyle (DASEL) conference at our church, which was led by Mark and Fiona Gilpin. They spoke about God's dream, getting free to enjoy evangelism and how God has designed us to be evangelistic. This conference was by far the most powerful and life-changing conference held in our church. We could feel the impact it had on everyone.

We as a church feel empowered to evangelise because of the conference. We didn't just see that we need to display his power, but that he has equipped us with everything we need to do the kingdom work, and that we are working together with him, to reach his dream. We feel unstoppable!

We were not used to seeing non-church people regularly attend our meetings, but after the conference we held a women's event and many non-church women from our area attended our church for the first time.

Shortly after the conference, we took a team of nineteen from the church to Iceland. Almost everyone shared words of knowledge, some had visions and others had dreams. Many people were healed, some people's lives changed from no hope to hopeful, from sorrow to joy. Three people became Christians.

If you need to empower your people for evangelism, then try DASEL you won't regret it.

Sámal Hanni Lognberg
Húsið Vón (House of Hope) Faroe Islands

GOD'S DREAM

A NEW PERSPECTIVE

Re-imagination is the birthplace for vision and change.
(Susan C. Young, Speaker and Author)

"I have been searching the Internet for months for the meaning of life."

We were buzzing as we travelled to the Midlands for an evangelism conference. It was a beautiful sunny day and we were enjoying the drive together. As we talked, we reminisced about our wedding day as the conference was being held in the church we got married in. Having arrived at our hotel, we booked a table for an early dinner.

As we ordered our food, we built rapport with the waitress and showed interest in her life. We often do this because God has a plan to do people good. He wants to involve us in what he is already doing in the lives of unbelievers. We find building rapport can help unbelievers be more open to what God wants to do for them and trust what we say. If we treat people with value, they are more likely to believe God values them.

During our conversation with the waitress God told Mark that she had a skin condition. We both regularly hear God speak to us about people around us. God speaks to us in different ways and we have had to learn how to hear him. We both hear God's voice in our mind, feel his heart for people, experience emotions that others may be struggling with or feel discomfort in part of our body that someone near us has real pain with. In this case Mark heard God's voice in his thoughts and simultaneously felt God's compassion for the waitress.

Mark asked the waitress whether she had a skin condition, even though there wasn't any visible evidence of this. To her surprise she said yes. Being young, she described her discouragement about needing to apply cream to her skin multiple times a day. Her skin was dry and sometimes caused significant discomfort, especially during the winter months when it would become sore on her face. Fiona offered to pray for her, which she gladly accepted. We both asked God to come and heal her skin and take away the irritation. After dinner we paid the bill, encouraged the waitress that God cared for her and went off to the conference.

The next morning, on Saturday, we went to breakfast and met the same waitress. She was *very happy* because her skin had been miraculously healed! She had a big smile on her face and was vibrant. God's healing had given her a new lease of life. We shared that God is good and that he loved her. This unbelieving waitress now knows God is real, cares about her and is able to heal her.

After finishing breakfast, we headed back to our room. We met another guest in the hotel corridor who was struggling to walk and was supporting himself with a walking stick. Feeling encouraged with how God had healed the waitress, we offered to pray for him. This guest revealed he had hurt his legs in a failed suicide attempt as he had tried to jump to his death.

God's compassion for him filled our hearts and we talked with him for a while. He wouldn't let us pray with him in that moment, but we did impart hope that his life had purpose and meaning. We said goodbye and set off to the conference.

On Sunday morning, Mark work up feeling the tangible presence of God as Fiona had woken earlier and was praying for him. Mark was feeling the love and closeness of God, which he often does during worship and evangelistic moments. Holy Spirit said to Mark, "When you check out of the hotel, pray for the receptionist to encounter me." This caught Mark by surprise, and he realised it would involve some courage to act on it! We discussed together how we might do this, and Fiona encouraged Mark to act on what he had heard.

After breakfast we checked out and had an opportunity to speak with the receptionist without anyone else around. We find unbelievers are more open to what God wants to do when they don't have an audience. Mark shared with the receptionist what God had said and offered to pray for her. What she said next caught us out because we were not expecting it.

The receptionist said, "I have been searching the Internet for months for the meaning of life but haven't yet found an answer." She shared it in a way that made it easy for us to tell her that Jesus was the answer. This is how God likes to work. He is working in unbelievers all around us and wants to involve us in the answers to their needs, prayers and questions. God has a dream to reconcile the world to himself and takes pleasure in inviting us to help him bring it about.

We then talked with the receptionist for about fifteen minutes about the meaning of life. During this time other hotel guests came to reception and checked out, but the receptionist wanted to carry on talking with us after each one left. At the end of the conversation we asked if we could hold her hand and pray for her. She accepted, so we both took her hand and prayed she would encounter God. We also prayed that she would know God was real, that he loved her, had a plan for her life and that she would feel his tangible presence.

We left the hotel, went to the last day of the conference and worshipped God in wonder. We were reminded afresh of how much God loves people, cares about them, wants to reconcile them to himself and delights to give us a part to play. At the close of the conference we went to talk to the main speaker, who was an evangelist, and asked him to pray for us because we wanted to be invited by God into more evangelistic moments. During such moments we feel close to God, feel his pleasure and sense this is one of the main reasons we are alive.

All these evangelistic moments happened in one weekend at our hotel. We didn't go looking for them, they happened as we went about our weekend plans. Holy Spirit, the person of God who resides in us and acts through us on the earth, initiated them all and invited us in to what he was doing in people whom we happened to be around. It doesn't matter where we are, which country we are in, whether we are working or on holiday, in routine or out of routine. There are always people around all of us who God wants to touch. What a privilege it is to be a Christian and know God's heart for the lost!

Our story

We both became Christians in our teens and met whilst studying at the same university. We quickly fell in love as we discovered a shared passion for fun, adventure, travel, Jesus, evangelism, and each other. Back then we had no idea just how well matched we were, given the journey God was going to take us on. We have been married for over twenty-five years and love the life we share. Both of us are so grateful for all that God has done in us.

This book tells the story about the journey God has taken us both on to discover how *he sees* evangelism. Our story has not always been straightforward because we have often had a different perspective about evangelism than others. We often found ourselves questioning common approaches to evangelism, without initially understanding why.

Over time we realised God was doing something new in us both. He had a story to tell about evangelism. Though this was a new story to us, it was not new to him. God was leading us on a journey to reimagine evangelism without the common hindrances and struggles that many can have when sharing their faith. God was introducing us to his story and to a new reality and perspective about evangelism.

During this journey we went through a time of self-discovery where we saw that God had given us both the evangelist gift. This surprised us both because the evangelist gift looks different in each of us, and it seemed to be integrated with each of our individual personalities and strengths.

We both found we loved hearing stories about the evangelistic adventures of other people. We loved hearing stories about how surprised Christians can be when God works through them in evangelistic situations, when they freely enjoy evangelism and when they discover how open people are to the gospel. We also found we loved stories about unbelievers being touched by the love, kindness, and healing power of God.

We found we wanted to spend time with people to encourage them in their evangelistic endeavours. We wanted to help people go further and be more successful in evangelism and to help people overcome any hindrances they had doing evangelism. We also wanted to impart any God-given strength we could to change the experience of evangelism into a positive experience for Christians.

Yet this did not seem to be the way others understood the evangelist gift. The common understanding seemed to be that the evangelist does all the evangelism, rather than helping others do it. During the early part of the journey it was difficult for us both when we had a view that was different to many Christians around us. Because we saw things differently, we were sometimes misunderstood.

We both had so many unanswered questions but could not deny the new perspective that God was developing in us. Despite thinking differently to many around us, we wanted to be faithful to what God was doing in us and began to share with those that were open to hearing what we had to say.

To our initial surprise, the new perspective God had given us on evangelism positively impacted people. We found the evangelist gift had the answers to the struggles many had with evangelism. Christians started to find motivation for evangelism and *wanted to do it*. For some, evangelism started to become enjoyable. Imagine that!

The new reality that God introduced to us is that evangelism does *not need to be difficult* for any Christian and is not something we have to struggle with. We can freely enjoy evangelism when we see it from God's perspective. Engaging in evangelistic moments that God invites us all into is a privilege and is something to look forward to.

During our journey we realised that our stories (as evangelists) can be an example to other Christians (who are not evangelists) of what an evangelistic moment could be for them. It was as if part of our evangelist gift could rub off on other Christians to help them become evangelistic. We have included our and other people's stories in this book to help you see what an evangelistic lifestyle can look like.

In this book, several of our friends also share stories of how they have embraced God's perspective on evangelism. Their stories include how evangelism changed for them and what it was like when God invited them into their first evangelistic moments. Their stories are honest, refreshing and full of encouragement.

Reimagining evangelism

We live in a day where more people are coming to Christ globally than at any other point in history. Yet evangelism is *not working for many churches and Christians*, especially in Western culture. Many Christians avoid it and don't think they can be any good at it. Some churches have little evangelistic engagement with friends, family, workplaces and communities, not realising God has answers for us.

Despite God designing evangelism to be a joy, privilege and adventure, many Christians, through bad experience and fear, have disengaged. Despite having an evangelistic identity, many Christians think evangelism is not for them. Even though God sets us up for evangelistic success, evangelism is not mainstream in many churches.

It is time to *reimagine evangelism.*

Imagine the passion that Jesus was feeling when he gave the Great Commission (Matthew 28:16-20).

Imagine the excitement and awe that the Apostle John was feeling when he saw the great multitude standing before the throne (Revelation 7:9-12).

Imagine every Christian knowing how God has uniquely designed them to be evangelistic.

Imagine every Christian freely engaging in evangelistic moments and having an evangelistic lifestyle.

Imagine Christians daily healing the sick among their neighbours, family, friends, work colleagues or complete strangers.

Imagine unbelievers encountering Jesus every day. Imagine people being saved and added to churches every day.

Imagine unbelievers wanting to find out about Jesus. Imagine Jesus having a good reputation among unbelievers.

Imagine evangelists helping people discover their evangelistic strength and the joy of supernaturally introducing unbelievers to Jesus.

Imagine there is no difference between the life of God that flows in church and the life that flows outside the church. Both are the same.

Imagine you don't need to organise any evangelism because life flows out of people wherever they are, whatever they are doing.

If you can reimagine evangelism in this way, then you are starting to see evangelism from God's perspective. You are starting to see evangelism as the early church experienced it. You are starting to see evangelism as churches have during historic revivals and awakenings. You are starting to see how evangelism could be for every Christian.

Original design

Let's go back to the first century church to see how they experienced evangelism. Acts describes how evangelism was for the early Christians. We encourage you to not just read the verses below but to also feel what evangelism was like for them.

Evangelism was a lifestyle and the church grew daily. The early Christians "preached the word wherever they went" (Acts 8:4) and the "Lord added to their number daily those who were being saved" (Acts 2:47). "More and more men and women believed in the Lord and were added to their number" (Acts 5:14). They "returned with joy" after doing evangelism (Luke 10:17).

Profound miracles happened regularly, that demonstrated the nearness and kindness of God: "People brought those who were ill into the streets and laid them on beds and mats so that at least Peter's shadow might fall on some of them as he passed by" (Acts 5:15). "God did extraordinary miracles through Paul, so that even handkerchiefs and aprons that had touched him were taken to those who were ill, and their illnesses were cured and the evil spirits left them" (Acts 19:11-12).

Evangelists brought joy to cities they travelled to: "Philip went down to a city in Samaria and proclaimed the Messiah there. When the crowds heard Philip and saw the signs he performed, they all paid close attention to what he said. For with shrieks, impure spirits came out of many, and many who were paralysed or lame were healed. So there was great joy in that city" (Acts 8:4-8).

God often spoke directly to Christians to invite them into evangelistic moments: "In Damascus there was a disciple named Ananias. The Lord called to him in a vision, 'Ananias!' 'Yes, Lord,' he answered. The Lord told him, 'Go to the house of Judas on Straight Street and ask for a man from Tarsus named Saul, for he is praying. In a vision he has seen a man named Ananias come and place his hands on him to restore his sight." (Acts 9:10-12).

So, why was their experience of evangelism so often different to ours?

Firstly, the early Christians did evangelism as Jesus did. They copied what they saw him do. They imitated his evangelistic lifestyle. Their method was Jesus' method. They didn't do anything differently to how he did it. Just like Jesus, they understood their mission was to "seek and save the lost" (Luke 19:10). The early Christians' experience of church included regularly seeing people saved.

Secondly, the early Christians "proclaimed the good news of the kingdom" (Acts 8:12). Jesus describes the Kingdom of God as a fine pearl that people will give everything for (Matthew 13:45-46). They did not preach a message that solely focused on conversion, but rather invited people to enter heaven's kingdom that can transform people and communities. The early Christians' message was not just words; they demonstrated the reality of Jesus' kingdom by miraculously healing the sick (Matthew 10:8). Their goal was to make disciples, not converts.

Thirdly, the early Christians understood that the Baptism of the Spirit (Acts 2:1-4) was given to enable them to achieve the Great Commission. They experienced a baptism that empowered them to see people saved. Joel's prophecy about the Holy Spirit being poured out on all people resulted in "everyone who calls on the name of the Lord will be saved" (Joel 2:32).

God's story

Can you imagine experiencing evangelism as the early Christians did? Can you imagine God inviting you into evangelistic moments on a regular basis? Can you imagine unbelievers encountering God as you pray for them?

God's story shows us that you can experience evangelism like the early Christians did, as this is how he designed it to be in your life. God's story also includes the answers to any struggles you may have with evangelism. God wants to change your experience of evangelism to be one of passion and adventure.

We invite you to reimagine evangelism with us.

GOD'S DREAM

GOD'S DREAM

Evangelism is selling a dream.
(Guy Kawasaki, Marketing Specialist and Author)

"I am completely better."

We were enjoying a meal together at our favourite hotel and restaurant in the town where we live. We had discovered the restaurant after one of our children won a competition to stay and eat there. Our child drew a picture of mum Fiona and they won first place! Since then we regularly enjoy breakfast, lunch or dinner there.

After finishing our meal, we went for a drink in the hotel bar. The bar was unusually quiet; we were the only people in it! Situations like this can be a clue that God is about to do something amazing. We got talking to the bar manager, who mentioned that the majority of the hotel guests that night were attending an evening wedding reception elsewhere.

As our conversation continued, God told Mark that the bar manager had pain in his back and legs. Mark heard God's voice in his thoughts and simultaneously felt God's compassion for the bar manager, because he was in pain.

Did you know that God knows the people around you? He knows

their life dreams, what they care about, any struggles they may have, any unanswered big questions they might want answers for, any pain they are in, and how they feel. He cares, because every person is his idea.

Mark gently asked the bar manager whether he had pain in his back and legs. He replied that he suffered from sciatica and had done for several years; he described the continual pain he had in his back and legs. He asked Mark how he knew he had pain in his back and legs. Mark replied, "I knew because God told me. He often speaks to me about people when I meet them because he wants to do them good. God cares about you and wants to heal you."

We offered to pray for him, and he accepted. Mark asked him whether he could put his hand on his shoulder to pray. He agreed and we both began to pray. In these situations we usually pray a short prayer, thanking God for the person we are praying for, affirming they are known and loved by God, and that he cares for them. We then ask God to heal the person. We pray with our eyes open and in a normal non-religious voice that does not draw attention to what we are doing or make the person we pray for feel uncomfortable. He thanked us for praying and went back to his duties.

A few weeks later we were back in the restaurant and saw the bar manager. We introduced ourselves and asked him if he remembered us. He did! Fiona asked how he was. He said, "I felt heat in my body when you prayed, and I am completely better." He had not had any symptoms of sciatica since! God set up the perfect evangelistic moment, with an empty bar, to bring healing to the bar manager. God does this because he cares about people and wants them to know how good he is.

We love being invited by God into evangelistic moments. We find it a privilege that God wants to include us in his longing to reconcile the world to himself. God wants to invite you into evangelistic moments tailor made for you. It is not only the evangelists that God invites into evangelistic moments; his invitation extends to all Christians, any time, any place, anywhere.

The greatest of all dreams

Do you have a dream? We do. In fact, we have many dreams. These dreams relate to our lives, our marriage, our children, our destiny, places we want to travel to and things we want to do. Some are already fulfilled, some are in the process of being fulfilled, and some have yet to be fulfilled.

For many years we wanted to take our children to see the Great Barrier Reef in Australia. We often watched documentaries on television about the reef and it captured the interest of our children. Travelling to the other side of the world can be expensive, especially with children and we have five! Yet God knew that dream was important to us and had a plan to bring it about.

After unexpectedly being made redundant in the 2008 UK financial crash, Mark took a new job at a loyalty company. What we didn't know when taking the job is that Mark would later qualify for additional employee benefits, including significantly discounted airline tickets. Without these, it would have been impossible for us to afford such a trip. In 2018 we took off from London Heathrow airport, with all five children on the plane. We both cried in gratitude to God that he had made our dream possible.

Richard Branson[3], businessman and philanthropist, says, "Dreaming is one of humanity's greatest gifts. It champions aspiration, spurs innovation, leads to change and propels us forward. In a world without dreams, there would be no adventure, no moon landing, no female CEOs, no civil rights. What a half-lived and tragic existence we would have. We should all dream big, and encourage others to do so, too."[4]

Dreams are important. God has wired us all to have dreams. Dreams show us what the future can look like. Dreams are deep passions and desires that long to be fulfilled. Fulfilled dreams fuel our sense of worth, significance, and reason for living. Fulfilled dreams make us feel his pleasure. In the Bible, King Solomon put it like this: "Hope deferred makes the heart sick, but a longing fulfilled is a tree of life" (Proverbs 13:12).

For the more significant dreams, we have learnt that we needed others to partner with us to see them fulfilled. They are often too big to achieve on our own. Having others partner with you to achieve a dream is part of God's design to bring them about. There are some dreams that we are not meant to achieve on our own. We are meant to help bring about each other's dreams.

At a conference Mark attended, everyone was asked to get into groups of three and share one or two items on their dream list. A dream list is things you would like to do and achieve within your lifetime. Mark got into a group with two friends in our church.

---

[3] en.wikipedia.org/wiki/Richard_Branson
[4] www.virgin.com/entrepreneur/richard-branson-why-dreaming-so-important-entrepreneurs

One of our friends had on his dream list to sit in a cockpit of a World War 2 fighter plane. Stored on Mark's phone was a list of all aviation museums in the UK, as a few months earlier he was talking with some work colleagues about possible days out for our children.

Only God could orchestrate that! Mark had on his dream list to tandem skydive. Our friend's sister happened to work for a company that did this. Coincidence or God-incidence? These are friends we have known for years but we did not know each other's dreams. Yet God had put the answers to each other's dreams within easy reach! Sharing our dreams with each other gave us the opportunity and privilege to be part of their fulfilment.

Did you know *God has dreams*? We know this, because we are made in his image (Genesis 1:27). If we have dreams, then God has dreams. He wants to share his dreams with us so that we have the opportunity and privilege to be part of their fulfilment. God wants to take part in fulfilling your dreams but also God invites you to take part in fulfilling his dreams.

God has *really big* dreams! He has designed the fulfilment of his big dreams to include us. More than that, he desires it that way. He could do it on his own, but he chooses to invite us into his adventures. There is one dream that God cares most about. The Apostle Paul describes it this way: "All this is from God, who reconciled us to himself through Christ and gave us the ministry of reconciliation: that God was reconciling the world to himself in Christ, not counting people's sins against them. And he has committed to us the message of reconciliation." (2 Corinthians 5:18-19).

God's dream is to reconcile the world to himself. This has always been his intent, desire, longing, and passion. That is a big dream!

In fact, there is no bigger or more important dream. The world's population is currently estimated to have reached 7.5 billion people. If you include all the people who have ever lived, that would be an even greater number.

God "wants all people to be saved and to come to a knowledge of the truth" (1 Timothy 2:4) and is patient with us "not wanting anyone to perish, but everyone to come to repentance" (2 Peter 3:9)[5]. God desires *all people to be saved*. Not a small number, but *all people*. That is people from every generation, every culture and every nationality.

In the book of Revelation, we see what the fulfilment of God's dream looks like:[6] "After this I looked, and there before me was a great multitude that no one could count, from every nation, tribe, people and language, standing before the throne and before the Lamb. They were wearing white robes and were holding palm branches in their hands. And they cried out in a loud voice 'Salvation belongs to our God, who sits on the throne, and to the Lamb.'" (Revelation 7:9-10).

The dream is celebrated with the words "Salvation belongs to our God." They are celebrating that God's *great dream* has come about. God is able to bring about his dream: a great multitude of people who will be reconciled to him. Praise is given for his wisdom, power and strength (Revelation 7:11-12). God is able to bring about his

---

[5] There are different ways to understand 1 Timothy 2:4 and 2 Peter 3:9, particularly from Arminian and Calvinist perspectives. Our intent here is to describe God's love, compassion, and desire for people to be saved. We do not include in this book a debate or comparison of the different theological viewpoints.

[6] Even though there is "a great multitude that no one could count", we know from scripture that not everyone will be saved, and some will go to hell (Revelation 20:11-15). It is important to distinguish between what God desires to see happen, what does happen and how these relate to his sovereign will.

dream: a great multitude of people who will be reconciled to him.

A new ministry

So how will his dream be fulfilled? God gives us the ministry of reconciliation. We are Christ's ambassadors and he makes his appeal through us (2 Corinthians 5:18-20). An ambassador is an important official that represents their country. They often speak for, advertise, and promote their country. Being an ambassador is seen as a privilege and a position of honour. God has made us ambassadors of Jesus and his 'country', which the Bible describes as his kingdom (Mark 1:15).

When we become a Christian we are born again (John 3:16) and become a new creation (2 Corinthians 5:17). Being a new creation includes being Christ's ambassador and having the ministry of reconciliation. We cannot separate this ministry from what it means to be a Christian. It is an integral part of who we are. That includes us, you, every Christian you know, even the ones who you think are least evangelistic.

God is inviting you to help him fulfil his big dream of reconciling the world to himself. It is not just the evangelists that get to take part in this adventure. It is all of us. God has woven you into his plan to fulfil his dream, where you take part in introducing people to him, where you get to reveal God's amazing kindness to others. This is the greatest privilege and invitation that you will ever receive: the privilege of doing something special and enjoyable.

Getting the right motivation for this new ministry is important. If Christians are not positively motivated, they are likely to struggle with evangelism. God's motivation is not fear, guilt, or condemnation. Rather it is an honour and privilege because we are his ambassadors.

The Apostle Paul describes his motivation for evangelism like this: "For Christ's love compels us, because we are convinced that one died for all, and therefore all died." (2 Corinthians 5:14). Jesus' sacrifice and death on the cross was for all people. This truth created a motivation of love for Paul and his companions. If we have God's love flowing in and through us, sharing our faith will be a joy rather than an onerous chore.

Paul has an amazing description of what love is: "Love is patient, love is kind. It does not envy, it does not boast, it is not proud. It does not dishonour others, it is not self-seeking, it is not easily angered, it keeps no record of wrongs. Love does not delight in evil but rejoices with the truth. It always protects, always trusts, always hopes, always perseveres." (1 Corinthians 13:4-7).

Knowing we are personally loved by God is part of what it means to be a new creation (2 Corinthians 5:17). When we are born again, we are given a new nature and identity. We become God's children (John 1:12) and experience Father God's love in our hearts (Romans 5:5). We are chosen by him and special to him (1 Peter 2:9). Knowing God loves us will help us engage in evangelistic moments.

It may take time to fully grasp how much God loves us and what it means to be his children. We can project onto God the imperfections of our parents. God is the perfect parent. He is flawless! We have learnt to primarily define ourselves by how God sees us. This is always more important than our own opinion and the opinions of others.

Any evangelism we undertake should always embody love.

During an evangelistic moment, an unbeliever should experience patience, kindness, hope, and honour. They should not experience embarrassment, anger, manipulation, or heartlessness. As ambassadors of Christ, we are representing Jesus to people. If we treat people with love, they will associate love with Christianity and therefore Christ. If we treat people without love in evangelistic moments, we are in danger of misrepresenting him.

Sometimes the motivation given for evangelism is that people are going to hell and we need to urgently do something about it. This may be true, but it doesn't necessarily make a good motivator for evangelism, because it induces fear or guilt or condemnation or any combination thereof! In the Bible, we do not see Jesus or the apostles systematically teaching hell as the primary motivator for evangelism.

If we see evangelism as an invitation to bring about God's dream, then we will see it as a privilege and adventure. If we are motivated by love and we see evangelism as a privilege, we will want to speak to people about the goodness of God and share his amazing ability to positively change their life. At any moment we will be open and willing for God to invite us into any situation he chooses.

God's love not only motivates us in evangelism, it is also the unbeliever's motivation for repentance: "Do you show contempt for the riches of his kindness, forbearance and patience, not realising that God's kindness is intended to lead you to repentance?" (Romans 2:4). This is God's design for evangelism: that his love and kindness bring people to repentance.

Evangelism that uses fear to bring people to repentance is not aligned to God's perspective. Jesus didn't frighten people into following him. Evangelism primarily needs to demonstrate the reality of God's love to unbelievers, so that they know he is good, that he cares about them, and that he is worth following.

If we disconnect evangelism from God's heart of love, we are likely to end up perceiving people as 'dirty rotten sinners' rather than people God loves. Also, the focus of our message is likely to be on sin and hell, rather than love and reconciliation. People are the object of his affection not his anger.

When we do evangelism, we usually feel God's presence and compassion for the person we are speaking to. What is happening here? God is sharing his love for the person we are speaking with. God is drawing us into his heart so that we feel for the person the same way he does. God will often tell us what he loves about a person so that we can communicate that to them. God may also reveal to us where they are in pain, physically or emotionally, so he can bring healing.

In these evangelistic moments there is an emotional bond between our Heavenly Father and us. As we join in his dream, we get to touch his heart and passion. We feel his love, hear his thoughts, and are touched by his desire to reconcile people to himself. When our children were younger, they loved to join in with what we were doing. Mark was once mixing concrete and laying paving slabs in the back garden. Without hesitation, our young children put their boots on, grabbed their spades from the sandpit and joined in mixing the concrete!

It is normal for children to want to join in with what their parents are doing. These shared activities create bonding moments between children and their parents, giving them a sense of closeness, belonging and purpose, as well as strengthening their relational connection. It is the same for us as children of God. We will take delight and pleasure to partner with our heavenly Father to bring about his dream. After all, reconciling people to God is the family business!

In his letter to Philemon, Paul writes, "I pray that you may be active in sharing your faith, so that you will have a full understanding of every good thing we have in Christ." (Philemon 1:6). If we are active in sharing our faith, we will grow as Christians and come to a better understanding of all that we have in Christ. That is the father's heart for us as we take part in the family business.

"I feel tingling around my ribs."

We were on a family day out in London, queuing to get into an attraction. The children were really excited because we were about to enter a Star Wars exhibition and they couldn't wait to get started! We had woken early to beat the queues and maximise our time together at the exhibition.

As we presented our tickets for the attraction Fiona noticed that the cashier was in some discomfort. We don't always need God to speak to us about unbelievers around us, as people's needs can be visible to our eyes. She asked him why he was in discomfort. We found out he had cracked his ribs in a recent cycling accident.

We built rapport with him by asking how he felt and showing interest in him. Fiona then offered to pray for healing, and he accepted. Fiona asked if she could hold his hand whilst she prayed. We both often do this because when we touch people, we often hear God speak to us about them. As Fiona prayed, the cashier said, "I feel tingling around my ribs," as God started to touch him. If people feel a sensation when we pray such as heat, peace, or tingling, it is often a sign that God is at work. We both started to get excited!

Mark then heard some words in his mind from Holy Spirit about what he loved about the cashier. When Holy Spirit speaks to us in our minds, it can at first seem like our own thoughts, but with practice, we can learn to discern whether our thoughts originate from God or ourselves. Holy Spirit does not only communicate to our minds, but also to our other senses.

When Holy Spirit speaks to us, he shares with us things about a person we couldn't have naturally known. This could be information about the person (e.g. their name), how God feels about them (e.g. compassion), what God loves about them (e.g. their creativity), what they may be concerned about (e.g. their health), their life dreams (e.g. what career they want to pursue) or what hinders them becoming a Christian (e.g. blaming God for a traumatic event in their life).

Mark shared with the cashier certain attributes of his character that God loved about him. Mark described what this young man cared about, his motivations, and things he did that God loved about him. Mark asked if what he said about him was true and he replied, "Yes, those things are really important to me."

The cashier was somewhat moved by this unexpected encounter. He was also encouraged and hopeful. We finished by affirming God's love for him and that God had a good plan for his life. During the process God was sharing his heart with us both for the cashier and his pleasure with us that we were partnering with God in his dream.

This evangelistic moment was a pleasure for the cashier and us.

Nobody had a bad experience or did not want to be there. God has designed evangelism to be like this.

Activation

We have added an activation section at the end of each chapter to help you reimagine evangelism and develop an evangelistic lifestyle. Through reflection, talking and listening to God, and practicing evangelistic moments, we invite you on a journey to experience evangelism as God intended. We encourage you to spend a few minutes at the end of each chapter working through the activation.

Reflect on this verse:

> *We are therefore Christ's ambassadors, as though God were making his appeal through us.*
> 2 Corinthians 5:20

Ask God:

- Will you share your passion with me for your great dream of reconciling the world to yourself?
- How do you want to motivate me to partner with you to bring about your dream?
- How can I know and experience more of your love?

Pray:

> *Father, thank you for the privilege of inviting me to take part in fulfilling your dream. Please fill me with your love and compassion for unbelievers around me, help me see them as you see them. Give me courage to share your heart with unbelievers around me.*

To do:

- Write down what God said to you and meditate on it.
- This week, whilst you are with people who are not Christians, ask God how he feels about them.

Further reading:

- Psalm 2:7-8
- 1 Timothy 2:3-6
- Romans 5:1-11

GOD'S DREAM

GOD'S PLAN

*Planning is bringing the future into the present so that
you can do something about it now.*
(Alan Lakein, Author)

"I am a survivor of the Holocaust."

It was our last night on holiday in Sydney. We had just finished
eating at the Opera House and were taking photos as the sun set
over Sydney Harbour Bridge. We had climbed the bridge a few
days earlier and had enjoyed the stunning views from the top, 134
metres up – it was a truly memorable moment.

As we started to walk back to our holiday apartment, the children
asked if we could buy some popcorn to eat during a movie we were
to watch later that evening. We spotted a convenience store, went
in, and chose some sweets and popcorn. As we were paying, Mark
had a thought in his head about someone having pain in their arms
and wrists.

Having a conviction that this was from God, Mark said, "Excuse
me, this question might seem unusual, but do you have any pain in
your arms and wrists?" The shop assistant looked a little confused
and said he did not. Mark then asked whether he had pain anywhere
else in his body. We do this because sometimes we discern people
have pain in their bodies but get the specific area of their body

wrong. He said he did not have any pain in his body. Mark was about to explain why he was asking such questions, when he heard Fiona speaking to another customer in the queue.

Fiona was watching what was going on and had a sense that God was inviting us into an evangelistic moment. When she heard that the shop assistant had no pain in his body, she wondered whether it was someone else that God wanted to heal. So, she asked the lady in the queue behind Mark whether it was her who had pain in her wrists, and she said yes. Part of the adventure of an evangelistic moment is finding the right person.

We introduced ourselves to this lady and asked if we could pray for her. She said she did not just have pain in her arms and wrists, but throughout her body because of arthritis. We offered to pray for her and she accepted. We held her hands and prayed that God would heal her. After we prayed, we walked out of the store and continued to talk to her and her husband.

She said to us, "I am a survivor of the Holocaust." Fiona said to the lady, "You have survived the Holocaust, so you know that there is a God in heaven don't you?" The lady replied, "Yes, but I feel guilty that I didn't die when my family and friends did." It is not uncommon for people to believe they had done something wrong by surviving a traumatic event when others did not. This is called survivor guilt[7].

When we pray for people in evangelistic moments, God touches them which can result in them opening up about their deepest needs. It often surprises us that people feel safe to talk to us in this

---

[7] en.wikipedia.org/wiki/Survivor_guilt

way, as we are strangers to them. Yet when God's presence touches people, his supernatural power transcends human etiquette.

This was the first time we had ever met someone who had survived the Holocaust[8] and we were somewhat in awe of this lady. We listened to her stories and affirmed that she had no reason to feel guilty. We said goodbye and continued the walk back to our holiday apartment.

As we walked, we talked about the evangelistic moment we had just had and what a privilege it was to meet someone who survived the Holocaust. We discussed how we could have prayed for her in person to be free of survivor guilt and wondered why we didn't take a moment to do so. In response, we decided to pray for her as we walked for God to bring freedom into her life.

After an evangelistic moment, our mind can have thoughts about what we could have said and done during that moment. Usually these thoughts are to teach us to grow in evangelism and to make more out of the next evangelistic moment God invites us into. We should not let such thoughts discourage us or let them make us feel condemned in any way.

We are still learning how to make the most of evangelistic moments. Our mindsets about how we learn and respond to success and failure affect how we grow in all areas of our life, including evangelism. Having a growth mindset[9] means we won't fear failure as we can learn and improve from failure.

---

[8] en.wikipedia.org/wiki/The_Holocaust
[9] Dr Carol Dweck, Mindset: The New Psychology of Success (2007).

A mindset is a set of beliefs we hold about ourselves. It will include how intelligent, successful, and able we think we are. If we hold a fixed mindset, we believe our intelligence and strengths are fixed traits that cannot change. If we choose a growth mindset, we believe that we can develop our intelligence and strengths, meaning we approach any opportunity with confidence that we can learn from it.

God has a plan

Have you ever planned a DIY project that took longer, and cost more than you originally thought? Even though you may have planned and budgeted for it, were there some unexpected things you didn't account for?

With the growing number of mobile devices in the house, Mark thought he would change two power sockets with new ones that included USB charging ports. Easy he thought! Just turn off the power, unscrew the sockets, connect the electricity cables to the new sockets, and screw them on. No problem, should be done within an hour!

It didn't work out like that. One socket would not fit in the kitchen because a tile had not been cut properly and was blocking the socket from being flush with the wall. In the front room, as Mark took out an old socket, the wall crumbled all around it. Both unexpected issues required additional unplanned time to complete the task.

When we plan, we cannot always account for the unexpected, even if we allow some contingency in our planning. God is not like that. He sees the end from the beginning. God has an extraordinary ability to plan! God is not caught out by the unexpected because he has seen it in advance.

H. G. Wells[10], writer and futurist, said, "We all have our time machines, don't we? Those that take us back are memories ... And those that carry us forward, are dreams." Dreams help us reimagine the future; planning to bring about a dream carries us forward to achieve them.

God has a plan to bring about and fulfil his dream. It is a good plan. God has planned for a successful outcome. God has thought through his plan. God knows his plan will work. God put his plan together before the creation of the world. God's plan also involves us (Ephesians 1:4 and 11).

Are you confident in God's plan?

Imagine it is around AD30 and God's salvation plan is unfolding as designed; the next significant phase is about to begin. Jesus has risen from the dead and is on a mountaintop with the disciples. The awe and excitement of his resurrection is still tangible. Hope and expectations are high. The unexpected twists and turns of the last three years are reaching a climax.

The disciples' minds are racing with memories of the many extraordinary miracles they have seen Jesus do. The disciples have such adoration and worship in their hearts towards Him. They are thinking what will happen now? What is Jesus planning next?

Jesus beckons to everyone. They anticipate from the expression on his face that he has something very important to say. He doesn't want anyone to miss it. He waits for the group to quieten down,

---

[10] en.wikipedia.org/wiki/H._G._Wells

until everyone is listening. He pauses for a moment just to ensure he has everyone's attention.

Then he says to them, "All authority in heaven and on earth has been given to me. Therefore go and make disciples of all nations, baptising them in the name of the Father and of the Son and of the Holy Spirit, and teaching them to obey everything I have commanded you. And surely I am with you always, to the very end of the age." (Matthew 28:18-20).

These are profound words. Jesus is giving his disciples the same mission he has. He is about to ascend to heaven and leave the responsibility of completing his mission to the disciples. Making disciples of all nations has just become *the* mission of the church, of which evangelism is intrinsically a part, including seeking and saving the lost (Luke 19:10).

Yet, not every Christian gets excited about this mission, particularly the evangelism part. Not everyone sees evangelism as an adventure or privilege. In fact, many Christians struggle with evangelism. Some think it is something others do. Few think it is something that they can grow and mature in. After all, who always gets excited about evangelism? *Jesus does!* He gets excited about every person who repents and becomes a Christian (Luke 15:7).

What was Jesus thinking when he invited each of us into his mission, which is commonly called the Great Commission? Was he thinking that we would love to help him fulfil his dream or that we would shy away from taking part? Did he think we would find it easy and be successful, or struggle and find it hard?

God knew what he was doing when he invited us to take part in fulfilling his dream. He had a plan to make it work. A plan for it to be successful. A plan where *we could be successful* at evangelism. A plan where *we can enjoy evangelism* without angst or striving.

The Great Commission is part five of a seven-part salvation plan. We like to call it the Great Invitation, because it is the greatest invitation anyone can receive. To understand whether part five of God's salvation plan is good and perfect, it needs to be viewed within the context of the entire plan.

Part 1 – Jesus' birth

Jesus' birth is so significant, there has never been or ever will be a birth like it. Conceived by the Holy Spirit and born to a virgin. Who else fulfils so many significant Biblical prophecies at their birth?

When Mary and Joseph took Jesus to Jerusalem as required by the law, they met Simeon who would not die before he saw the Messiah. He took Jesus in his arms and said, "My eyes have seen your salvation, which you have prepared in the sight of all nations: a light for revelation to the Gentiles, and the glory of your people Israel." (Luke 2:30-32).

Jesus' birth is an indispensable part of God's salvation plan. Part one of God's plan was for him to be born a human being and live among people. Jesus was called Immanuel, meaning God with us (Matthew 1:23). God did not ignore the plight of humanity; he stepped into it so he could rescue us from our sin!

Part 2 – Jesus' life

Who else's life can compare to Jesus' life? He came as God incarnate. Even from a young age he amazed the teachers in the temple with his understanding (Luke 2:41-51). Jesus' life revealed God in a measure that had never been seen before: "Don't you know me, Philip, even after I have been among you such a long time? Anyone who has seen me has seen the Father. How can you say, "Show us the Father"?" (John 14:9).

Jesus also modelled to us a life dependent on Holy Spirit, showing us how to believe in him for miracles: "It is the Father, living in me, who is doing his work. Believe me when I say that I am in the Father and the Father is in me; or at least believe on the evidence of the works themselves. Very truly I tell you, whoever believes in me will do the works I have been doing, and they will do even greater things than these, because I am going to the Father." (John 14:10-12).

Jesus' life is an indispensable part of God's salvation plan. Part two of God's plan was for Jesus to show us what the Father is like (John 17:25-26) and how to have a father-child relationship with him. Rather than an angry and distant God, Jesus reveals a God who is loving, kind and in reach of everyone.

Part 3 – Jesus' death

Who else has a death like Jesus, becoming the redeemer of the world? Jesus is described as the "Lamb of God, who takes away the sin of the world" (John 1:29). Jesus' death provides payment for all sin (1 Peter 2:24). People no longer need to be separated from God by their sin (Matthew 27:50-51).

Jesus' death makes a way for us to be reconciled to God: "Since we have now been justified by his blood, how much more shall we be saved from God's wrath through him! For if, while we were God's enemies, we were reconciled to him through the death of his Son, how much more, having been reconciled, shall we be saved through his life! Not only is this so, but we also boast in God through our Lord Jesus Christ, through whom we have now received reconciliation." (Romans 5:9-11).

Jesus' death is an indispensable part of God's salvation plan. Part three of God's plan was for Jesus to die for the sin of the world, taking our punishment, so that we may receive forgiveness (Romans 3:23-26). Jesus' death demonstrates and proves his love for sinners who were unable to save themselves (Romans 5:6-8).

Part 4 – Jesus' resurrection

The resurrection of Jesus is unique; it brought victory over sin and death. The resurrection means death no longer needs to be feared (Hebrews 2:14-15). God now becomes our father, "I am ascending to my Father and your Father, to my God and your God" (John 20:17).

Jesus' resurrection enables us to live a life not ruled by sin, "For if we have been united with him in a death like his, we will certainly also be united with him in a resurrection like his. For we know that our old self was crucified with him so that the body ruled by sin might be done away with, that we should no longer be slaves to sin – because anyone who has died has been set free from sin." (Romans 6:5-7).

Jesus' resurrection is an indispensable part of God's salvation plan. Part four of God's plan was to free us from sin, so we could become new creations and the righteousness of God (2 Corinthians 5:17, 21).

Part 5 – The Great Commission

The Great Commission comes here. Note its context: it comes between Jesus' resurrection and ascension. This is hugely significant and we will shortly explore it further.

The Great Commission is an indispensable part of God's salvation plan. Part five of God's plan is where he invites us into his dream of reconciling the world to himself by giving every Christian a new ministry (2 Corinthians 5:18-20).

Part 6 – Jesus' ascension

After giving the Great Commission, Jesus ascends into heaven. The ascension demonstrates Jesus' authority: "Who has gone into heaven and is at God's right hand – with angels, authorities and powers in submission to him." (1 Peter 3:22) and his return to the Father in heaven (John 16:28).

Paul described it this way: "He raised Christ from the dead and seated him at his right hand in the heavenly realms, far above all rule and authority, power and dominion, and every name that is invoked, not only in the present age but also in the one to come. And God placed all things under his feet and appointed him to be head over everything for the church, which is his body, the fullness of him who fills everything in every way." (Ephesians 1:20-23).

Jesus' ascension is an indispensable part of God's salvation plan. Part six of God's plan is to place Jesus over all things and give him authority to complete the Great Commission (Matthew 28:18-19).

Part 7 – Giving of the Holy Spirit

Once Jesus ascended to heaven, he asked the Father to give the promised Holy Spirit (John 14:15-17). John the Baptist links this event with Jesus and describes how he will baptise with "the Holy Spirit and fire" (Luke 3:16).

The Holy Spirit came and rested on believers: "When the day of Pentecost came, they were all together in one place. Suddenly a sound like the blowing of a violent wind came from heaven and filled the whole house where they were sitting. They saw what seemed to be tongues of fire that separated and came to rest on each of them. All of them were filled with the Holy Spirit and began to speak in other tongues as the Spirit enabled them." (Acts 2:1-4).

The giving of the Holy Spirit is an indispensable part of God's salvation plan. Part seven of God's plan was to share Jesus authority with us (Luke 9:1-2) and empower us to represent Jesus to the world (Acts 1:8). The baptism of the Holy Spirit enables us to do signs and wonders (Acts 14:3) and complete the Great Commission.

The deliberate plan

God's salvation plan was deliberate. The Apostle Peter tells his fellow Israelites that Jesus "was handed over to you by God's deliberate plan and foreknowledge; and you, with the help of wicked men, put him to death by nailing him to the cross." (Acts 2:23). Each part of the plan was carefully considered and intentionally chosen.

God has an integrated plan, one point flows into the other. God's plan is only complete when considered as a whole. All seven parts of the plan are indispensable. The Great Commission is no less important than the other parts. It is important to observe where the Great Commission fits within the plan:

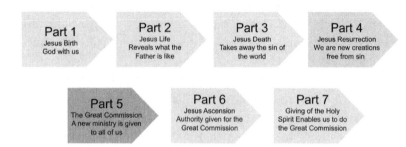

The Great Commission fits between the resurrection and ascension. The Great Commission starts with "All authority in heaven and on earth has been given to me" (Matthew 28:18). Jesus is linking together his power and authority from his resurrection and imminent ascension, with his invitation for us to take part in the Great Commission, so that his dream can be fulfilled.

This is a victorious king saying, 'I have all that is needed to fulfil my dream!' He has authority over sin, sickness, and every dominion because he will (shortly) be seated at the right hand of God. This is the context of Jesus commissioning us for his mission, which incorporates evangelism.

Jesus is not thinking that we will struggle, but rather that we will be successful, because he has all that we need to be successful. He has empowered us and shared his authority with us by baptising us in the Holy Spirit. Jesus has designed every Christian to be successful in evangelism. It is a set-up!

Whilst in exile in Babylon, Daniel has a dream about the future moment where he sees Jesus being given all authority. Jesus isn't only given authority; he is also given a kingdom (Daniel 7:14 NKJV). This is significant because it influences how we share the gospel, which we explore in a later chapter.

God has thought the plan through. This is his only plan: salvation is found only in Jesus (Acts 4:12). His plan is not flawed. In fact it is perfect, it will succeed. He has done all the hard work for it to happen. His life, death, resurrection, invitation, ascension and giving of the Holy Spirit makes it superbly achievable.

He is looking for us to say 'yes' to his Great Invitation to help fulfil his dream. Involving us in his plan is genius because God can invite believers across the globe into thousands of simultaneous evangelistic moments. By working through his worldwide church, his plan is achievable because a global harvest will occur.

"Do the names Andrew and Emily mean anything to you?"

We had really enjoyed being away to celebrate our 25th wedding anniversary; our two-week holiday was coming to an end. We were sitting talking with other holidaymakers as we waited for our bus to arrive to take us to the airport.

Fiona started talking to one married couple about how their holiday had been and they asked us about ours. During her reply, Fiona spoke about our wonderful friends from church who were looking after our five children whilst we were away. Dropping something about our faith into a conversation can spark an evangelistic moment.

This led to a conversation about the wife's mother, who from her description was a loving, spirit-filled Christian who impacted many in her village. As she spoke, we could tell she marvelled at her mum's faith but did not feel she could have it herself. Her mum had recently died and shortly before had written a personal letter to everyone in her village.

During the conversation Mark began to realise this was an evangelistic moment and wondered what God might want to do. At that moment he heard Holy Spirit say the names in his mind 'Andrew and Emily.' Sometimes we will not know if thoughts in our mind are from God unless we share them! So, Mark asked the couple, "Do the names Andrew and Emily mean anything to you?"

The wife thought for a few minutes and said she did not know any couples called Andrew and Emily. Mark felt a little disappointed, but he suddenly thought the names did not necessarily mean they were a couple, so he asked did either of the names mean anything to them. The wife said yes because her name was Emily! She did not know an Andrew, but we were excited because Mark got one name right!

We then shared with her how God knew her name, that she was his idea and was valued by him. It impacted her that God knew her name. Our bus then arrived, and we travelled to the airport. Our hope is that this started a journey for her of discovering she could know God in the same way her mum did.

Activation

Reflect on this verse:

> *You will receive power when the Holy Spirit comes on you;*
> *and you will be my witnesses in Jerusalem, and in all Judea*
> *and Samaria, and to the ends of the earth.*
>
> Acts 1:8

Ask God:

- Are there any reasons why I am not excited about evangelism?
- How do you want to involve me in your salvation plan?
- How have you empowered me to bring in the harvest?

Pray:

> *Father, I accept your invitation to take part in fulfilling*
> *your dream. Thank you that you have planned for your*
> *dream to be successful. Please fill me with your Holy Spirit*
> *to empower me for evangelistic moments. Teach me to*
> *recognise your voice when you speak to me.*

To do:

- Write down what God said to you and meditate on it.
- This week, whilst you are with people who are not Christians, ask God what he loves about one of them.

Further reading:

- Ephesians 1:1-14
- Acts 2:1-12
- 1 Peter 1:10-12

GOD'S DREAM

ME ... EVANGELISTIC?

Embrace what makes you unique.
(Janelle Monáe, Singer and Actress)

"I feel full of light on the inside."

It was mid-afternoon on a Friday. Mark was working from home and he had a couple of hours more work to do before the weekend began. It had been a long week at work, he was feeling tired and he was looking forward to the weekend starting.

The doorbell rang. Mark opened the door to find two charity workers asking for financial support for their organisation. They introduced themselves as Julie and Sarah. Mark politely listened to them, with the intent of finishing the conversation quickly, so he could get back to his work. It was not that their cause was unworthy; Mark was just focused on finishing his work so he could start the weekend.

As Mark was listening to the charity workers, God spoke to him in his mind about one of them. He also wondered whether she was a Christian. He asked, "Julie, are you a Christian?" "Yes," she said. Mark continued, "God can see the dreams you have, he is watching over them to bring them about."

As Julie heard this, her eyes began to water. This was an

encouragement from God that was important for her to hear. She thanked Mark and briefly shared some of her dreams. Whilst they were speaking, the other charity worker, Sarah, was listening intently to the conversation, amazed at what she was hearing. Sarah asked Mark, "How do you do that?"

Mark explained that he could hear God speak to him through the Holy Spirit and the conversation led on to a discussion about being baptised in the Spirit. As they talked, Sarah realised there was more to being a Christian then she had experienced to date. There was a hunger developing in her to encounter God in a new way. Mark asked her, "Do you want be baptised in the Spirit now?" Sarah said, "Yes."

Mark and Julie then prayed for Sarah to be baptised in the Spirit there and then on the doorstep! Mark asked if he could hold Sarah's hand and continue to pray. We always ask permission before we pray for someone or touch him or her in some way, such as holding their hand or putting our hand on their shoulder. We also find that God often speaks further to us about a person when we touch them.

Mark asked Sarah, "How do you feel?" "I feel full of light on the inside," she replied. When we pray for people, asking them what they are experiencing is important as it can indicate how God is working in them. They may feel peace, heat, encouragement, or a conviction that God is real. They may also hear God in their thoughts, as he may want to speak to them about something in their life.

As Mark took Sarah's hand, Holy Spirit said to him that she had a boyfriend who would draw her away from her faith. This is one way that God commonly works in Mark. God will often speak to him about specific things in people's lives that will stop or hinder them becoming a Christian, or preventing them growing as a Christian.

When we hear God speak to us about someone else, it can be helpful to turn it into a question and explore with him or her what it means. Mark asked Sarah, "Do you have a boyfriend?" As he said this, Julie looked amazed and astonished. This confirmed to Mark that he was on the right track. Sarah then spoke about how her boyfriend was not good for her and Mark replied by sharing what Holy Spirit had said.

Sarah was initially surprised but listened intently. Mark explained what a good boyfriend would do and how he should treat her. They spoke further about what it meant to follow Jesus and change her life so she could become a disciple of him. Julie and Sarah both thanked Mark for this unexpected God moment and went on their way amazed and encouraged.

Mark was not looking for this opportunity, in fact his mind was on completing his work. Yet God had orchestrated this moment and invited Mark into it. God loves to invite us all into evangelistic moments.

Mark's story

My mum was an evangelist. She was a good example to me of what the gift looked like. She spent much of her time befriending people on the edge of society and at the edge of church, showing them Jesus. She modelled a confidence in the gospel to transform lives.

In my teens I realised I had an affinity with her because I was also an evangelist, though I did not fully understand what it meant back then. In my teens I remember I would cry that people would die without coming to know Jesus. I felt compassion for those who were lost. I would often dream of everyone in the church taking part in the Great Commission.

During my university holidays I attended evangelism events in Europe and found affinity with others there. At the time I didn't understand why I couldn't find the same affinity with everyone in my church. I now understand that most people who attended those events in Europe were most likely to be evangelists.

At university I was baptised in the Holy Spirit (Acts 19:1-7) and supernaturally grew in my evangelist gift. A boldness and courage started to grow in me; I started to hear God's voice in evangelistic situations. I began to research the evangelist gift and read widely about revival and biographies of evangelists throughout church history.

I began to see God's design for the evangelist gift. I was amazed as I read the revival stories of evangelists and started to wonder why they did not seem commonplace today. I began to think whether we had fully grasped evangelism from God's perspective. I had so many questions, but few answers.

In the early years of our married life, we settled in a great church in the southeast of England. Our evangelist gifts were recognised, we ran Alpha[11] Courses, saw people saved, trained people in supernatural evangelism and started to see evangelistic momentum in the church.

---

[11] www.alpha.org, Alpha is a course that is designed to help people explore what is means to be a Christian. Alpha courses are run in over 100 countries, with over 24 million people having taken the course.

Yet something was wrong in me. I started to resent my gift. In fact, I would regularly complain privately to God about the evangelist gift that he had given me. I would say, "Why have you given me this gift? Why can't I have another gift? Why have you given me the worst of all the gifts? Why can't I be a teacher or a prophet?"

One of the reasons I complained to God was that my strength in evangelism seemed to remind some of their struggle with it. Though they loved God deeply and knew how important evangelism was to God, many had not been able to find solutions to their evangelistic struggles. My gift seemed to be a blessing to some and a stumbling block to others. One person called my evangelistic enthusiasm 'scary'. For many Christians in the western church, the word 'evangelist' may have unfortunate connotations and negative associations.

Then it all changed for the better. I encountered God in a way I didn't expect at a conference. During the conference one of the speakers spoke about all the gifts listed in Ephesians 4: the apostles, prophets, evangelists, pastors, and teachers. He described their importance and how they are related. I had never heard anything like that before; it gave me a new perspective. The speaker spoke about the way God had value for the evangelist gift in a way that I didn't.

God has chosen to give gifts of people to the church to create maturity and unity. Paul describes it as follows: "So Christ himself gave the apostles, the prophets, the evangelists, the pastors and teachers, to equip his people for works of service, so that the body of Christ may be built up until we all reach unity in the faith and in the knowledge of the Son of God and become mature, attaining to the whole measure of the fullness of Christ." (Ephesians 4:11-13).

The gifts listed in Ephesians 4 are God's design and method to enable the church to reach the whole measure of Christ and represent him fully to the world. These gifts help fill the gaps in Christians understanding and practice. People with these gifts can create healthy churches that grow and build themselves up in love. Having people with all five gifts active in churches will increase the growth and momentum of God's work.

The Ephesians 4 gifts are different to gifts of the Holy Spirit that are for individual Christians.. These gifts are given for the common good and include prophecy, serving, encouragement, giving, mercy, wisdom, knowledge, faith, healing, miraculous powers, distinguishing between spirits, speaking in tongues, and interpreting tongues (Romans 12:6-8, 1 Corinthians 12:4-11).

Later at the conference during the worship, I sensed Jesus standing in front of me. He began to paint my face with what looked like war paint; this was happening in a vision. The war paint was vibrant and full of colour and to me represented a *recommissioning* in the evangelist gift. The way Jesus painted my face felt unique and personal to me. It was like he was communicating that the evangelistic gift in me had a unique expression.

It was as if God was communicating to me that my evangelist gift is like a warrior[12], someone who is experienced and brave. I often feel courage during evangelistic moments, feeling God's strength and power. I can also impart courage to others when they do evangelism with me.

I intensely felt the love of God. Jesus said to me, "I love your evangelist gift, it is my gift and it is my pleasure to give it to you." I

---

[12] The comparison of the evangelist gift to a warrior in the vision was an analogy and does not infer a war against people, see Ephesians 6:10-17.

started to cry. Jesus then said, "I love who you are, how I made you and what I am turning you into – you are my design." I cried some more!

This encounter changed my perspective on the evangelist gift and how I see myself. I now understand that God designed the evangelist gift and therefore it is glorious, valued and to be celebrated! I now understand that God has designed it to equip and bring freedom to people who struggle with evangelism and being evangelistic.

A new journey of wonder began as I started seeing things differently. I now love being an evangelist! I even now joke it is the best gift because I get to introduce people to Jesus. It is now my passion to motivate and equip Christians to be evangelistic. For me there is no better thing. Knowing how God sees me has set me free to be who he designed me to be.

Being evangelistic is in our spiritual DNA

The Apostle Paul spoke about Christ in us. He described the glorious riches of the gospel as, "Christ in you, the hope of glory" (Colossians 1:27). He described about how, now that we are Christians, Christ lives *in us*. He then provides the purpose of this, that God "was pleased to reveal his Son in me so that I might preach him among the Gentiles" (Galatians 1:15-16).

Part of God's salvation plan is putting Christ in us, so that he is revealed to unbelievers around us. For the Apostle Paul it was the Gentiles, for the Apostle Peter it was the Jews (Galatians 2:7). When Christ lives in us, one of the ways that works out in our lives is that we become evangelistic. God wants to reveal his son in you to unbelievers around you. God works in us to fulfil his good purpose (Philippians 2:13).

Being evangelistic about God's dream is in the spiritual DNA of every believer. God has wired every believer with an inherent ability to share the gospel. You may not have thought that it is possible that every believer can be evangelistic. It is, yet many Christians do not think they have a natural ability to be evangelistic.

We understand there are several reasons why this may be the case. It is not uncommon that only a few Christians in churches are actively and confidently engaged in personal evangelism. Others have had negative experiences of evangelism, which has put them off doing it. Some have not learned how to overcome fear. Others have been poorly motivated by evangelists, leaving some feeling guilty and somewhat condemned for their lack of evangelism.

It is important to realise that being evangelistic is not the same as being an evangelist, any more than being prophetic is the same as being a prophet. The evangelist equips people, so they become evangelistic; in the same way a prophet equips people to be prophetic. Evangelists are not looking to clone themselves, but rather to awaken the evangelistic DNA within others so that they can effectively share and demonstrate the gospel in a way that is unique to them.

In the English language we add the suffix 'ic' to a word to mean having some of the characteristics of or pertaining to[13]. For example, someone who is described as poetic has some of the characteristics or nature of a poet but is not himself or herself a poet. Similarly, being evangelistic means you share some of the characteristics of an evangelist, but you are not necessarily an evangelist.

---

[13] www.dictionary.com/browse/-ic

Consider your uniqueness

We have all been "fearfully and wonderfully made" (Psalm 139:14). God has not made anyone like you. In the entire history of the human race there will never be another person like you. Your uniqueness deserves to be celebrated. Your combination of the way you look, personality, gifts and abilities make you unique.

You are also made in the image of God (Genesis 1:27). You uniquely demonstrate something of God's love and character in a way that no one else can. God has uniquely designed you to be evangelistic. Being evangelistic is part of your identity; you will express this differently to how other people do.

Po is the hero in the movie Kung Fu Panda 3[14]. Whilst he is thinking about how he will train an army in martial arts, he recognises that everyone will fight uniquely. He says to his trainees, "Your real strength comes from being the best 'you' you can be. So, who are you? What are you good at? What do you love? What makes you, 'you'?"

Your evangelistic strength will be linked to your other strengths; it is not separate to the rest of you. In fact, it is integrated into your core being alongside that which makes you 'you'. When God designed you, it included how he would reveal his Son through you. We can see this in the Bible: people expressed their evangelistic nature differently.

---

[14] en.wikipedia.org/wiki/Kung_Fu_Panda_3

The creative

"I have filled Bezalel with the Spirit of God, with wisdom, with understanding, with knowledge and with all kinds of skills – to make artistic designs for work in gold, silver and bronze, to cut and set stones, to work in wood, and to engage in all kinds of crafts." (Exodus 31:3-5).

This Old Testament example provides us with insight as to how the Spirit of God works in people. In Bezalel, there is a link between being filled with the Spirit and his wisdom and skills. His way of making known the mystery of God was to use his creative skills and craftsmanship to design the Tabernacle and its contents.

God wants to make himself known through your creativity. You may be good at art, music, dance, writing or other creative expressions. God wants to reveal his son, Jesus, through these strengths. Some people encounter God through prophetic art; others may find Christ through music or novels.

Just because you may feel that certain traditional methods of evangelism (such as door-to-door) are not for you, does not mean that you are not wired to be evangelistic. Being evangelistic is linked to your strengths such as creativity. This is what being evangelistic could look like in your life.

The charitable

"In Joppa there was a disciple named Tabitha (in Greek her name is Dorcas); she was always doing good and helping the poor." (Acts 9:36).

Tabitha was known for doing good and helping the poor. You may be drawn to those who are socially marginalised or disadvantaged. You may volunteer for charity work. There may be a specific group in society that you are drawn to. You may be generous and hospitable. If you have a heart for those who are destitute of wealth, influence, position, or honour, then God may want to make himself known to them through your kindness.

At times in history the church has separated evangelism and social action. They are not meant to be separate. God cares about the body, mind, soul, and spirit. Helping the poor is a core part of what it means to be a Christian[15]. This is what being evangelistic could look like in your life.

The storytellers

"Then, leaving her water jar, the woman went back to the town and said to the people, 'Come, see a man who told me everything I've ever done. Could this be the Messiah?' They came out of the town and made their way towards him.'" (John 4:28-30).

The Samaritan woman encounters Jesus at the well, and he answers her questions, reveals her needs, introduces himself as the Messiah and tells her the Father is seeking her. This impacts her so greatly that she becomes evangelistic to those in her town.

Our testimonies are an invitation for unbelievers to encounter Jesus. God wants to make himself known through our stories. You may be good at telling stories. If you can hold an audience whilst

---

[15] Jesus and the apostle's ministry incorporated the poor, examples include Matthew 25:31-46, Luke 4:18, Luke 6:20, Luke 12:32-34, Luke 14:12-14, Luke 19:8-9, James 2:3-6, Galatians 2:9-10.

storytelling, this may be what being evangelistic could look like in your life.

The professionals

"As Jesus was walking beside the Sea of Galilee, he saw two brothers, Simon called Peter and his brother Andrew. They were casting a net into the lake, for they were fishermen. 'Come, follow me,' Jesus said, 'and I will send you out to fish for people.' At once they left their nets and followed him." (Matthew 4:19-20).

Jesus says to fishermen that if they follow him, he will teach them to catch (fish for) people. It is like Jesus is saying, I can take your trade, all your training, everything you are good at, your life experience and use it to bring people to faith.

Many Christians have professional experience and a trade. Our life experience is varied, but we have all learnt lessons on the way. God wants to reveal his Son Jesus through your life and work experience. The two flow together, this is what being evangelistic could look like in your life.

How has God uniquely designed you?

When we equip Christians, we encourage them to ask God how he has uniquely designed them to be evangelistic. This is one of our favourite ways of equipping because it can be the most transformational. Christians discover how God has uniquely designed them to partner with him to be evangelistic. They realise that being evangelistic is in their spiritual DNA. It is something they already have, that just needs to be recognised, encouraged, and developed.

Once they discover this, they come alive to being evangelistic and a new journey of adventure begins. They embrace taking evangelistic opportunities, often with surprising results, finding that Father God sets them up for success. Suddenly it becomes natural and is something they want to do. Being evangelistic is no longer beyond what they think they are capable of.

Teaching people pre-packaged gospel presentations can be helpful, but it doesn't teach people how they are designed to be evangelistic. To put it another way, it doesn't release the inbuilt evangelistic DNA they have within their God-given identity. Linking being evangelistic with people's identity is transformational.

Corrine

I often share Jesus' compassion with people at my workplace and God showed me this is one way that I am uniquely designed to be evangelistic. I decided I wanted to share with unbelievers what God loves about them. I did this with a colleague at work who was deeply impacted by what God thought about her. I also wanted to learn to listen to Holy Spirit and pray for healing for someone. Whilst I was on a train God spoke to me about a health condition that another passenger had.

Though I wanted to share this, I was a little reluctant as the whole carriage was full of passengers. I prayed for God to help me share what he had given me. Not long after as the train stopped at a station, all the passengers in the carriage got out except for me and the lady opposite who God had spoken to me about! I then took the opportunity to share and pray with the other passenger. I am learning to introduce Jesus to the people around me and understanding that God sets me up for evangelistic success.

Maria

When I asked God how he had uniquely designed me to be evangelistic, he spoke to me about how he had designed me to flow evangelistically out of intimacy and dance to a rhythm of his heartbeat. This impacted me because I love dancing.

God also set me free from a lie I believed about my ability to do evangelism many years earlier when I was a student at university. During a university mission I was the only student in my friendship group not to see someone become a Christian. Following this experience, I believed I was no good at evangelism, which I now know not to be true.

I am now free to be myself in evangelistic situations and I am starting to recognise the moments where God is inviting me to partner with him in his dream to reconcile the world to himself.

Renewing our mind

You may need to go on a journey to gain an understanding of what it looks like for you to see yourself as evangelistic and increasingly adopt such a lifestyle. Part of this process will involve renewing our mind to see evangelism the same way God does. To renew our minds means to transform our thought patterns to become more like the way God thinks, giving up our belief systems that are different to his (Romans 12:1-2).

If you have renewed your mind in another area of your life, how you thought and believed, then the journey may be similar for evangelism. The journey would most likely have involved meditating on scripture, getting prayer, and learning from people who were further down the road than you, and asking yourself why your thinking, beliefs and experience didn't line up with Biblical truth.

For example, a Christian goes on a journey from viewing their identity as a 'worthless sinner' to seeing themselves from God's perspective, as a royal son or daughter who is loved and valued (John 1:12, 1 Peter 2:9). This journey will involve changing perspective from feeling guilt, condemnation, powerlessness, insecurity, and hopelessness to feeling love, freedom, security, confidence and knowing they have a God-given destiny.

A similar journey is required if you do not believe you are uniquely designed to be evangelistic. This journey involves changing perspective, so you no longer think that evangelism is not for you or that it is difficult. Neither should it generate fear in you or cause you to think you won't know what to say in an evangelistic moment. Your renewed mind then believes that being evangelistic is part of your God-given identity, that you can make the most of evangelistic opportunities, that sharing your faith becomes a positive experience and that *being yourself* is the best way to be evangelistic.

To change our thinking requires us to give time to reflect and reinforce in our minds the Biblical truth that we don't yet believe. As you meditate on Biblical truths, challenge your own current thinking, renewing your mind where you need to. Ask Holy Spirit why you struggle to believe. It may even help to acknowledge and be honest about what you don't believe and then say out loud what the truth is (Romans 10:9). Speaking it out will help to start changing what you believe about being evangelistic and evangelism.

Then put into practice what you are learning. Learn from how it goes and practise again, growing each time. As you do this, you can learn to be aware of your thinking before, during and after an evangelistic moment. As you discern your own thoughts, you can then choose what to believe, aligning your thoughts to the Biblical truth. This helps avoid falling back into old thought patterns.

Monitor your own thinking and watch how it changes, acknowledging the progress you are making, celebrating even the smallest changes. Let Holy Spirit be your teacher and he will lead you into the reality of every truth (John 16:13). Depend on the Holy Spirit rather than formulaic methods as you grow in what it means to be evangelistic.

If you have learnt to drive a car, how did your first lesson go? When driving for the first time, many people will not change gears smoothly. They may stall the car, brake too sharply and over or under steer. It takes time to learn to drive. The same is true of being evangelistic. Over time, we can become more competent and confident, relying on Holy Spirit.

Embracing what it means to be evangelistic allows us to develop an evangelistic lifestyle in which we can succeed and thrive. Being evangelistic is part of who we are. We don't reserve being evangelistic for a few events or opportunities.

"The pain started 48 hours ago."

Mark was travelling abroad with his friend David, as they had both been invited to speak at a conference. After clearing airport security, they headed for a café to get breakfast. A waitress came over to take the order. God then spoke to Mark in his mind about the waitress having pain in a specific area of her neck.

Mark asked her if she had pain in her neck and pointed to the place on his neck that God had highlighted. To her surprise she said yes and asked how he knew that. Mark explained that God had told him because he cared for her and wanted to heal her pain. David offered to pray for her to be healed, which she accepted. After prayer, she left to process the order.

After finishing breakfast, Mark and David decided it was time to go to the departure gate. As they left the café, the waitress came over and said thank you because her neck pain had gone and she had full movement back in her neck! Mark and David were encouraged by God's goodness to the unbelieving waitress.

As they reached the flight departure gate, it was unusually quiet for an international flight; there were very few passengers around. Mark wondered whether God might invite them into another evangelistic moment. As Mark approached a flight attendant to show them his boarding pass, he felt pain in his calf muscle.

There was nothing wrong with Mark's leg, so he knew God was telling him that the flight attendant may have pain in her leg. This is one way God can speak to us; he can give us temporary discomfort in our body to communicate to us where someone else is suffering real pain.

He asked her whether she had pain in her calf muscle. It is always helpful to ask a question, because we may not fully understand what God is saying. It maybe her, or somebody she knows that has the pain. She replied, "Yes, the pain started 48 hours ago, I am quite worried about it, how did you know about it, are you a doctor?"

Mark explained that God cared for her, knew her concern and wanted to heal her. She began to cry because she had not told anyone about it and realised in that moment that God cared for her. She had a church background but nothing like this had ever happened to her before.

Mark then asked to take her hand, which she accepted and as he prayed the pain significantly reduced. Mark then noticed that other flight attendants and airport security staff were quietly watching. At this point Mark decided it would be wise to politely end the conversation and board the aircraft. He did not want to draw any unnecessary attention to the flight attendant.

Being aware of the environment during an evangelistic moment is important, as we do not unintentionally want to cause concern or embarrass the person we are with. As Mark took his seat, he felt the pleasure of God for accepting his invitation into the evangelistic moment. Mark and David had three further evangelistic moments throughout the flight!

Activation

Reflect on this verse:

> *I praise you because I am fearfully and wonderfully made;*
> *your works are wonderful, I know that full well.*
> Psalm 139:14

The Bible encourages us to declare out loud what we believe (Romans 10:9). It may be helpful to say out loud the following truths:

- I am God's idea; he has uniquely designed me to be evangelistic.
- Being evangelistic is in my DNA, it is natural for me to share my faith.
- It is a privilege when God invites me to partner with him in evangelistic moments.

Ask God:

- How have you uniquely designed me to be evangelistic?
- Please give me some opportunities this week to share my faith, based upon how you have designed me to be evangelistic?
- As Christ is in me, to whom around me do you want to reveal your son?

Pray:

> *Father, thank you that I am fearfully and wonderfully*
> *made. Thank you that you have uniquely designed me to*
> *be evangelistic and it is part of my identity. Please teach me*
> *to express this strength and enjoy the evangelistic moments*
> *that you want to invite me into.*

To do:

- Write down what God said to you and meditate on it.
- This week, be attentive to God, looking for evangelistic moments that he wants to invite you into.

Further reading:

- Acts 10:44-46
- Galatians 2:20
- James 2:5

GETTING FREE

I've learned that fear limits you and your vision. It serves as blinders to what may be just a few steps down the road for you.

(Soledad O'Brien, Journalist and Producer)

"Ask him about his Sweetheart."

Fiona was visiting a church for the weekend to do evangelism training and take the church out to do outreach. On the Friday night whilst spending time with the youth group, a local homeless man wandered into the church building. He was known to the church and dropped in to bring some cakes to say thank you for how kind they had been to him on several occasions.

His intent was to give everyone in the church some cake. The youth leaders explained there were over a hundred people in the church. The man looked a bit worried at this point and exclaimed, "I have only brought a few cakes. There won't be enough for everyone!"

A church member brought him a cup of coffee and they sat with Fiona and started chatting. The man began to speak about his problems with alcohol and how poor his health was because he smoked too much. Fiona offered to pray for his severe respiratory condition, to which he replied, "Why on earth would you? It's my own fault."

Fiona talked to him about how God wants to bring healing and freedom, even when the situation we are in is our own fault. That is the nature of God's grace and mercy. In response, he shook his head and was quite dismissive. During an evangelistic moment it is helpful to ask God where to go next.

Fiona asked God to give her something to share with the man. Instantaneously, a thought popped into her head. She knows it is God, when the thought comes too quickly for her to have made it up herself! Also, as on this occasion, hearing words or phrases that are not common to modern parlance. The thought was, "Ask him about his Sweetheart."

So she did! "Tell me about your Sweetheart." At this point the man began to weep. He talked about a tragic accident many years ago when his sweetheart had died of drowning and he blamed himself for her death. Fiona felt God say in her thoughts that it was not his fault.

She communicated this to him, and he sobbed. She repeated it several times. Fiona's conviction at this point was that this was the start of his drinking problem. Fiona spoke with him about God's love, forgiveness, mercy, grace, and Jesus' invitation for a fresh start. The man was very touched and thankful and let Fiona hug him.

God knows people's real needs, often buried within their hearts and emotions. Yet this can be what Holy Spirit wants to heal during an evangelistic moment. We have learnt not to shy away from people's emotional pain, but to partner with God to bring about healing and restoration.

Fiona's story

When I first became a Christian in my late teens, I read the Great Commission in the Bible and I understood that it was my and every other Christian's job description. It didn't even occur to me that any other Christians might have a different understanding of that verse. I thought the normal Christian life involved Bible reading, prayer, worship and being an active witness.

As a young Christian, I went to a Reinhard Bonnke event in Birmingham; he was an evangelist who saw millions of people come to Christ in Africa[16]. I was hugely impacted by his passion for the gospel, and of his regularly seeing miracles and healing. I can still remember the message he preached. I felt the power of his message: a call to every Christian on the planet to be a part of bringing in the harvest.

At university I was asked to be the Evangelism Outreach Secretary for the Christian Union Executive Committee. I was surprised at the time but looking back I now see that some people saw what God was doing in me more clearly than I then did. During my first year at university I led my sister, a student in my accommodation block, and a student on my course to Christ. Sharing my faith was natural to me.

In my twenties I volunteered for charities working with drug addicts and alcoholics, always looking for an opportunity to talk about Jesus. I believed the gospel had the power to rescue and transform people from destructive lifestyles. In my thirties I was part of the Alpha Team at my church and saw more people become Christians. At this point in my life I really wouldn't have described myself as an evangelist.

---

[16] www.cfan.org.uk

It was in my early forties that I started to realise I was an evangelist. During this time, I was a student at the Eastgate School of Spiritual Life[17] (ESSL) and evangelism was a weekly part of the course. I enjoyed evangelism, but also started to realise that some students struggled with evangelism and some tried to actively avoid it!

I took part in an ESSL weekend mission team and was asked to do some outreach training for the church we were visiting. The couple I stayed with were very pastoral, but at the end of the weekend said, "We can do that, we can find people to talk to, that God wants to bless and touch their lives."

I saw people at the church go through a process that started with the thought, "Evangelism is not for me" and ended with the thought, "Yes I can do that". I realised I had an ability to equip people for evangelism and help them get rid of unhelpful emotional 'baggage' they may have picked up though discouraging or difficult evangelism experiences.

On the Monday morning following the weekend mission team, Kim Carter, one of the Eastgate Church leaders rang me. My instant reaction was, "Oh no, why would a church leader ring me Monday morning on their day off? There must be something wrong!"

Kim said, "I have just been on the phone to the church leader where you have been on mission and they wanted to pass on their thanks for a great weekend. They said you were a brilliant evangelist. You made it fun, engaging and inspired many to go out."

---

[17] ESSL runs Daytime and Evening schools, whose aim is to equip and deploy followers of Jesus Christ to radically change society through a naturally supernatural lifestyle of signs and wonders. For further information visit eastgate.org.uk/essl

It made me think, was I an evangelist? Why would the church leader say that? What was it that I said, did, modelled and displayed, that caused them to think I was an evangelist? Even though others clearly saw I was an evangelist, the lights did not come on for me until someone pointed out to me what my gifting and calling was.

I started to become more self-aware of the evangelist gift at work in me. The following year, I started to lead outreach at ESSL with another student. During my third year at ESSL as I was regularly teaching students how to do evangelism, it became apparent that many Christians for one reason or another shy away from evangelism. After digging a little deeper, I realised that this was mostly due to past bad experiences of evangelism or fear of doing evangelism.

To address this, I started using principles to deal with emotional wounds and lies. Emotional wounds can occur in evangelism when Christians are asked to do something they didn't want to do, found it uncomfortable or cringey, or felt coerced into taking part in some form of organised outreach activity. Emotional wounds can also occur when a leader's talk made a Christian feel guilty or condemned for not doing enough evangelism.

When we are wounded emotionally, we can end up believing a lie about ourselves, God, or other people. It can make us cynical or hard-hearted. In the context of evangelism, Christians can believe lies about their evangelistic ability or God's ability to help them with evangelism.

I would lead students in prayer to forgive people who had emotionally wounded them. I would pray for students to be healed from their emotional wounds. I started to encourage students to get free from previous negative evangelism experiences.

During these sessions with students, Holy Spirit would reveal emotional wounds and lies they had believed about evangelism, often for years. Students began to find freedom in evangelism as they responded to Holy Spirit and worked through their 'baggage' related to this.

I also started to address fear, that students did not need to 'grit their teeth' whilst doing evangelism. I started to teach them that there was a better way, to help them see that God's "perfect love drives out fear" (1 John 4:18). Students found freedom from fear and bad experiences and started to *enjoy* evangelism.

Freedom started to grow in other areas as well. Students got free from lies such as 'I am not good at evangelism' and they stopped comparing themselves with others. This had a noticeable impact on the willingness of students to engage in outreach activities and their subsequent evangelistic testimonies that followed. More and more students began to see God impacting the lives of people they encountered in outreach activities.

This led to a significant reduction in the reluctance of students to engage in evangelism. As time progressed, students would share more testimonies about how they had evangelistic opportunities outside of ESSL contexts, and gradually, for more of them, it started to become part of their everyday lifestyle.

I have learnt that it is not enough for evangelists to just teach people evangelism techniques, how to hear Holy Spirit's voice and how to pray for healing. Evangelists also need to bring freedom to people's evangelism-related emotional wounds, lies and fear-based issues.

Once Christians are free, they can enjoy evangelism and develop an adventurous evangelistic lifestyle.

Freedom to enjoy evangelism

Freedom is defined as the power or right to act, speak or think as one wants[18]. Jesus does not just bring us freedom from sin (Romans 6:22), but a life of freedom: "it is for freedom that Christ has set us free" (Galatians 5:1). Jesus' freedom is not temporary: "So if the Son sets you free, you will be free indeed." (John 8:36).

When we become Christians, God's desire is to set us free from anything that stops us being the people God designed us to be, so that we can wholeheartedly follow him without any hindrances. The freedom that Jesus bought us includes not being enslaved or imprisoned by bad experiences or lies about evangelism. Also, it means not being inhibited, feeling self-conscious, or bound by fear of people, what they think of us or how they respond to us.

If you are struggling with evangelism, then there are God-provided truths and answers. God did not design evangelism to be something you would struggle with. God wants to set you free so that you can enjoy being evangelistic and confidently engage in evangelistic moments.

Knowing God's love means that we don't have to live with fear, because, "There is no fear in love" (1 John 4:18). Fear of man is a snare; it can trap us, keep us in a place of pain, create inertia, kill momentum, and stop us moving forward in any area of our life, including evangelism (Proverbs 29:25).

---

[18] en.oxforddictionaries.com\definition\freedom

The Biblical truth is that God "has not given us a spirit of fear, but of power and of love and of a sound mind." (2 Timothy 1:7 NKJV). Despite the Apostle Paul's imprisonment, Christians became confident in God and proclaimed the gospel without fear (Philippians 1:14).

You can be evangelistic and do evangelism *without fear*. We don't have to do evangelism through gritted teeth and suppressing unhelpful emotions. His presence and his love can abide in us, so there is no room for fear. If fear stops you engaging in evangelism, you can ask God for his perfect love to drive out the fear. If we see ourselves as beloved children of the God of love, fear does not need to dominate our lives.

Within evangelistic moments, it is natural sometimes to feel a little nervousness. When Holy Spirit speaks to us about an unbeliever, we may at times feel a little reticent before we share it. At other times we will feel no nervousness at all. These are normal human emotions that we can control in the moment. When we speak about fear, we are talking about fear that prevents us from doing evangelism.

If you struggle with fear in evangelistic moments, it maybe that a negative experience has opened your life to fear. If that were the case, we would encourage you to seek freedom through a counselling ministry. Issues in one area of our lives can flow into another area, such as evangelism. An example of this could be if someone struggles with rejection, they don't want to do evangelism in case they are rejected by people.

Unforgiveness can also stop us doing evangelism. Forgiving people who have hurt us brings us freedom from emotional pain or a sense of injustice. We are encouraged to forgive and to, "Bear with each other and forgive one another if any of you has a grievance against someone. Forgive as the Lord forgave you." (Colossians 3:13).

We have heard many stories of Christians being asked do some type of evangelism that they did not really want to. Some felt manipulated into doing it, others felt awkward and embarrassed, and some felt they had to do it through a sense of responsibility. Such experiences have left some Christians with a negative association of evangelism.

Regardless of their motives and intentions, forgiving those who may have put us in these situations can bring freedom to engage afresh in evangelistic moments. God can heal any negative or difficult memory of evangelism. God's desire is that you experience evangelism as he designed it.

Jess

At the beginning of the Evening ESSL school year, I put the dates for the all-day Saturday events in my diary except for the evangelism one, because I was determined to be busy that day so I didn't need to attend!

On the Wednesday night before the Saturday, I attended Evening ESSL as usual, even though Fiona was giving a talk about evangelism to help prepare the students for the Saturday outreach. I decided to go anyway because all the other talks had been interesting, even though I thought that evangelism is really not me.

During Fiona's talk, I began to get stirred in my spirit about the Great Commission, God's dream, his heart for those who don't know him and how he wants us to partner with him so we can share his love with those who are lost. I realised that I needed to repent of my attitude, because it was based on fear.

After the talk, I spoke to Fiona and said I haven't booked into the Saturday Evangelism event, but I really feel like I want to. Fiona said it was not too late and I was more than welcome to attend and join in with the outreach.

Saturday started to loom, and I began to have second thoughts about attending. I thought I could just turn up and if I felt really uncomfortable, I would just leave.

I turned up and enjoyed the worship and teaching but was still not convinced I was going to go out and do the afternoon outreach. I was thinking that I would just sneak off after lunch!

I did decide to stay and got put in a group with one of Mark and Fiona's evangelist friends, Angela. I thought I would go out and just shadow Angela and the others in the group, secretly determined not to speak to anybody.

Angela helped make my group's evangelism accessible, possible, and fun. Throughout the afternoon outreach, I found that God had gone before me and even though I found myself in evangelistic situations I had previously not chosen to put myself in, I was able to freely speak to people and share the gospel with them.

I still remember the outreach I did on the ESSL Saturday evangelism event. In all my years on earth, it was one of my best days ever and I just loved it! I am now enjoying evangelistic moments as I share the gospel with people around me in my everyday life.

Peter

After initially trying out the Daytime ESSL taster day, I really wanted to attend the school, but there was a big 'but': I really didn't like the idea of the weekly evangelism. Determined not to be put off, I concluded that the sessions would probably only last for a short time and, surely, I would be able to opt out of anything I didn't like!

So, just a few weeks into the ESSL term I remember, having received evangelism training from our enthusiastic evangelism leaders, the dreaded time came: the first outreach. I may have looked calm but really, I was a wreck. And for the next few weeks nothing much changed, but here's the wonderful thing: after only a couple of months I really started to like it and look forward to it.

The testimony and help from other students, the encouragement from the evangelism leaders and just weekly 'practice' began to change things. At the same time, the teaching in ESSL built up my sense of identity and the confidence that we did indeed carry God's presence with us, to bless, pray for, heal, and encourage the people we met. It helped me that the evangelism leaders always emphasised that having a go and taking a risk was applauded by God.

After overcoming my fear there was no going back. There were wonderful opportunities to demonstrate the love of God to unbelievers through prophesying and words of encouragement. People I spoke to often experienced more of a touch of God's love than I expected.

Doing evangelism turned out to be a joy rather than an embarrassing activity – always fun and sometimes a serious moment of connection with people who really needed to experience a touch of God's love. As I reached the end of my time at ESSL, some of my best memories were from doing the evangelism. It was training for life and I wouldn't have missed it for the world!

Common lies about being evangelistic and evangelism

There are lies about evangelism that we find are often believed by some Christians. We empower what we believe. Tony Robbins[19], author and life coach, says, "If you tell yourself a lie long enough, you'll start to believe it." If we believe untruths about evangelism, we will feel disempowered about doing it. If we believe Biblical truths about it, we will feel empowered to do it.

"It's not my gift, I am not any good at evangelism, there are others who can do this much better than me, I should leave it to them."

Being evangelistic is not a gift; it is a ministry every Christian is given when they become a new creation (2 Corinthians 5:16-19). We all have the same invitation and privilege to partner with God to bring about his dream. We are all sent by Jesus, as he was sent by the Father (John 20:21).

We can do all things through Christ who gives us strength (Philippians 4:13). Whilst sometimes it may not work out as we anticipate, truth is not defined by our experience. We can learn to be evangelistic and be good at evangelism, if we take time to practice and increase our dependency on God.

We are successful if we share with someone what Holy Spirit has told us. We are successful if we show God's kindness. It is helpful to

---

[19] en.wikipedia.org/wiki/Tony_Robbins

define your success based on how you partnered with God: that you took a risk, stepped out in faith, were obedient, and not solely on how the person responds.

God desires everyone to come to repentance and reconcile the whole world to himself. We are all invited to participate because more harvesters are needed (Matthew 9:37-38). God's divine power has given us all we need for a godly life, including evangelistic moments (2 Peter 1:3). Our uniqueness enables us to reach specific people that others may not be able to.

"Evangelism is hard, evangelism is for extroverts, and my stories don't sound that great compared to others."

In the book of Acts, people were saved daily (Acts 16:5). We live in a time where more people are born again daily worldwide than at any other time in history. Evangelism is easier than we think when we recognise that we are empowered by Holy Spirit (Acts 2:17-21). We are chosen and appointed to bear fruit (John 15:16).

Jesus' gifts are given by his choosing and not based on personality type. Evangelists can be introverts (e.g. Mark) or extroverts (e.g. Fiona). Psychological definitions of extrovert and introvert are based upon where someone gets their energy and where they put their attention. It has nothing to do with supernatural gifting!

The testimony of God's work in each of our lives is very powerful (Revelation 12:11). Our personal stories can have a positive impact on others. What God has done in our lives is a testimony to what he wants to do again in others. All our stories are important and can impact unbelievers.

"I am not confident I hear God well enough to share with unbelievers. I won't know what to say if I am asked a difficult question. Sometimes fear just gets the better of me."

Hearing God's voice is not a gift, it is a Christian's birthright (John 10:3-5). We can all hear God in an evangelistic moment; he has designed us that way (John 10:27). We all at times may not recognise God's voice, but the truth is that the voice of God is powerful (Psalm 29:4). It may be that we just need to practice hearing or need some help to differentiate his voice from our own thoughts.

Holy Spirit will remind us of what to say during evangelistic moments (John 14:26). When we testify about Jesus, he will give us words and wisdom to speak (Luke 21:13-15), so we don't need to worry beforehand about what to say. It can be helpful to ask Holy Spirit for the reason that someone is asking us a question. There are many reasons for asking a question, including general interest, wanting a logical answer, personal suffering, to test us, or another reason.

We are encouraged to always be prepared to give an answer for the hope that we have (1 Peter 3:15-16). If you don't know what to say in an evangelistic moment, ask Holy Spirit for inspiration. Affirm the person you are speaking with as an important human being, loved and valued by God. If nothing does come to mind, politely say you don't know the answer.

During ten years of running Alpha Courses we have had many lively discussions with unbelievers. A key to seeing many of them become Christians was being able to answer their questions with God's revealed wisdom in the moment, or being reminded by Holy Spirit of things we had previously read or prepared in advance.

The Holy Spirit does not make us fearful or timid (2 Timothy 1:7). God's love drives out fear. The Bible regularly encourages us to not be afraid and have courage. Holy Spirit said to the Apostle Paul, "Do not be afraid; keep on speaking, do not be silent." (Acts 18:9).

Jesus promised to be with us as we share the gospel (Matthew 28:20). Jesus did not show any fear when he shared the gospel with others. Evangelism can be done confidently and without any fear; we can live a life free from fear and anxiety.

"It feels rude to interrupt people going about their everyday life. If I get it wrong I will look really stupid. I don't want to get rejected."

God often interrupts people as part of their conversion process and he doesn't consider it rude (Acts 9:1-9). Biblical truth is not based on cultural 'norms', but rather on God's 'norm' of an advancing kingdom (Matthew 11:12).

Interrupting people can be done with politeness, gentleness and building rapport. It does not have to be perceived as rude (1 Peter 3:15). Punctuating someone's day with an encouraging word, praying for healing, bringing love, a random act of kindness or giving him or her peace, hope or comfort is a welcome interruption!

We are encouraged to practice spiritual gifts so that we progress and mature (1 Timothy 4:15). Unbelievers we speak to have little expectation about what will happen and are unlikely to respond badly if you get it 'wrong'.

We have many stories where someone did get the 'wrong' prophetic word, or someone didn't get healed immediately after prayer. In most of these cases people still encountered God because they felt valued and loved. Success in evangelistic moments can still happen, even when we perceive we got it 'wrong'.

Some people will reject Jesus, we may be hated because we belong to Jesus (John 15:18-19). If this happens, we are to 'shake the dust of our feet' (Matthew 10:14). By this Jesus means we are to not take on the responsibility of their response or to personally feel rejected.

"I am not seeing my own answers to prayer so I can't pray for someone else. My life or character doesn't measure up to be a 'good Christian witness'. They look like they have got their lives together, do they really need Jesus?"

Paul regularly saw miracles, but his own illness did not stop him preaching the gospel (Galatians 4:12-14). Our personal circumstances do not limit God's ability to work through us as, "We know that in all things God works for the good of those who love him, who have been called according to his purpose." (Romans 8:28).

There is no end to the increase of the kingdom (Isaiah 9:7). Our prayers are powerful and effective (James 5:16), through the righteousness of Christ, not our own. There is no condemnation for those who are in Christ (Romans 8:1). Our imperfections do not change our identity as children of God. We are a new creation and we are his witnesses (Acts 1:8).

We are introducing Jesus and his gospel to unbelievers; we are not introducing them to our ability. We share our faith because we are invited to partner with God, not because we may, or may not, be living in the measure of maturity that we aspire to.

Jesus is seeking those who are lost, from every people group in the whole world (Revelation 7:9). In the Bible, people are saved from all parts of society – for example, tax collectors and prostitutes (Matthew 21:31) and prominent men and women (Acts 17:4).

People's relative standing in society or how well they seem to be managing their lives is not the real issue. God has chosen when each person is born in history so that they will reach out and find him (Acts 17:24-27). God wants to reconcile all people to himself.

"What ... earrings like these?"

Sometimes Fiona and a local youth worker, Nick, go out on Friday nights looking for the opportunity to speak to young people hanging about on the streets and in local parks. They ask God for 'clues' to lead them to specific people who God wants to speak to. They are confident that God is seeking the lost and will show them where to find them.

When praying, prior to going out, various names, locations and other seemingly random items popped into their heads. They wrote these things down on a piece of paper. The 'clues' included 'Gemma', 'Diamond Earrings', 'Star' and 'Angel'. They then left and found themselves on a path called 'Angel Walk'.

They saw three girls sitting nearby on a bench. They began chatting with them and Fiona asked if any of them was called Gemma. A very surprised longhaired girl said yes. Fiona explained that they were Christians, learning to hear from God. She told them that prior to coming out they had asked God for some information to lead them to people who he wanted to bless, heal and do good.

Fiona asked Gemma whether she owned a pair of diamond

earrings. She pulled back her long hair and said, "What … earrings like these?" Fiona said yes, she was excited that this evangelistic moment was unfolding. Gemma smiled and explained that they were real diamond earrings; a gift she had received for her eighteenth birthday. Encouraged by this, Fiona asked, "Do stars have any significance for you by any chance?"

Gemma went on to explain that she had been having many conversations with her mum about God. Her mum had a colleague at work that was a Christian who had been sharing her faith with her. The colleague had invited her mum to church on several occasions and she was undecided whether to go or not. Gemma remarked that only a few days prior she had stood in her bedroom, looked up at a star and said, "God, if you are real, come and show me."

Fiona said, "We don't want to big ourselves up, but I think we are the answer to your prayers!" Fiona and the youth worker talked to her about Jesus, encouraged her to go to church with her mum and her mum's colleague, and gave her a copy of John's Gospel. They also prayed for a second girl who had a painful swollen leg, after which the swelling was visibly reduced. All three girls were shocked and pleasantly surprised.

We commonly find that we are part of an ongoing story where God is already working in someone's life. God has the amazing ability to invite multiple Christians at different points in time to be involved in someone's journey of salvation. What a privilege it is when we are invited to play a part.

Activation

Reflect on this verse:

> *It is for freedom that Christ has set us free. Stand firm, then, and do not let yourselves be burdened again by a yoke of slavery.*
>
> Galatians 5:1

Ask God:

- What lies am I believing about being evangelistic and evangelism?
- What truths do you want to give me in exchange for these lies?
- If I have had a negative experience of evangelism, is there anyone who I need to forgive?

Pray:

> *Father, thank you that you love me and do not want me to live in fear. Please fill me with your love and drive out any fear that I have. Show me your peace during evangelistic moments. Help me see how you have equipped me to be evangelistic.*

To do:

- Write down what God said to you and meditate on it.
- This week, whilst you are with someone who is not a Christian, share a testimony with them about God's goodness towards you.

Further reading:

- 1 John 4:13-18
- John 8:34-36
- 2 Timothy 1:6-9

GOD'S DREAM

JESUS' MESSAGE

The only source of knowledge is experience.
(Albert Einstein, Physicist)

"Excuse me, do you have a painful shoulder?"

We were flying home with our team following an evangelism conference we had run. During the flight, Mark and Fiona both independently felt pain in their shoulder. Neither of them had any issues with their shoulder, so began to think that this was God speaking to them about someone around them with a shoulder problem that he wanted to heal.

Fiona turned to the passenger next to her and asked, "Excuse me, do you have a painful shoulder?" but they replied saying no it was fine. Later in the flight, when the air hostess was serving coffee, Fiona asked her whether she had a painful shoulder but she did not. Fiona asked if any of her flight crew colleagues happened to have a painful shoulder, but none of them did.

After we landed, we headed towards the 'Meet and Greet' Car Parking. As Mark began speaking with the car parking attendant, Fiona realised it was late at night and this would be the last person she would see before she got home. So, she asked him, "Do you have a painful shoulder?" He replied, "Yes"!

Sometimes we need to search for the person who God wants to touch. It may not be someone in our immediate environment, but could be someone we meet later in our day. The parking attendant shared his story about how many months ago he had injured his shoulder at the gym. He spoke about the months of physiotherapy he had gone though, the regular pain he was in, and his limited mobility.

Fiona explained that whilst she had been on the plane, she had felt pain in her shoulder and it was because God wanted to heal his shoulder. She asked him whether she could pray for him. Despite being somewhat surprised he agreed to be prayed for. Fiona asked if she could hold his hand and pray and he accepted.

After prayer Mark asked him if anything had changed. He was not expecting anything to happen. Mark encouraged him to move his arm to see if God had done anything. As he moved his arm, he was able to fully rotate it without any pain. He looked so shocked and surprised!

When we pray for healing, sometimes God heals as we pray. At other times he heals after we prayed, when someone tests to see what has happened. When Peter took the hand of the lame beggar at the temple gate, his legs and ankles instantly became strong (Acts 3:7). Getting people to test their bodies after prayer can reveal a miracle. There will be some medical conditions that cannot be immediately tested and may require confirmation of healing from a doctor.

He then said, "What have you done to me?" and looked a bit suspicious as if it was a trick. Sometimes when we pray for people, they can go through a range of emotions. He was not sure what had happened, but we explained that we were Christians and affirmed that Jesus had healed him, loved him, and wanted to do him good.

He then asked what kind of church we were from, as he was not used to seeing miraculous healing. We explained this was normal to us and that God wanted to show him his kindness. We left him encouraged and pain-free as we headed to our car for the drive home.

The gospel of the kingdom

Have you ever wondered what is the best way to share the gospel? There is no one more amazing than Jesus, so how do we introduce people to him? When Zacchaeus the wealthy tax collector met Jesus, it transformed him. He decided to give half of his possessions to the poor and repay anyone four times what he had cheated them. This is amazing for a person whose life is centred on wealth!

Jesus described his kingdom using an analogy of treasure that people would sell all they had to obtain it (Matthew 13:44). Jesus and his kingdom are an incomparable treasure that is worth seeking after and obtaining. Jesus' gospel is about his kingdom and how it is within reach of everyone. Jesus does not simply want to rescue people from hell. He wants to transform their lives.

Terms like 'Christian', 'Christianity' and 'becoming a Christian' obviously did not exist when Jesus shared the gospel. The first recorded use of the term 'Christian' is in Antioch, which was approximately in AD 42 (Acts 11:25-26). The term Christian was first used over ten years after Jesus' death, resurrection, and ascension. The early Christians were also known as 'the Way' (Acts 9:2). Terms like 'the Way' and 'Christian' were primarily used to describe people who followed Jesus. They were not used to explain the gospel.

The term gospel[20] means to announce, bring, and show good news. It is the origin of the word evangelise, which means to talk about how good you think something is[21]. In the New Testament, its contextual use is the good news of God's kindness, the coming of the kingdom of God, and his salvation obtained through Jesus.

In the New Testament (NIV UK), the term 'gospel' and 'good news' are used 122 times and the terms 'Kingdom', 'Kingdom of God' and 'Kingdom of Heaven' 124 times. Putting these terms together, they refer to Jesus' message – *the good news of the kingdom*. Jesus' message was, "The time has come. The kingdom of God has come near. Repent and believe the good news!" (Mark 1:14-15).

The term kingdom[22] announces the realm of the royal power of a new triumphant king. Marvin R. Wilson, a leading scholar on Christian-Jewish relations, states, "In Hebrew thought the kingdom is wherever God sovereignly takes charge and rules in human affairs." [23]

It is a realm where Jesus has all authority in heaven and earth (Matthew 28:18), including authority over all sickness (Matthew 8:8-9). He rules this realm from where he is seated: "far above all rule and authority, power and dominion, and every name that is invoked, not only in the present age but also in the one to come." (Ephesians 1:21).

When Jesus spoke about his kingdom realm, people experienced it, for example through miraculous healing of every disease and illness

---

[20] euaggelizō, Strongs G2097 and euaggelion, Strongs G2098
[21] dictionary.cambridge.org/dictionary/english/evangelize
[22] basileia, Strongs G932
[23] Marvin R. Wilson, Our Father Abraham: Jewish Roots of the Christian Faith (1989), Page 181.

(Matthew 4:23). Jesus said the reason he was sent was to proclaim the good news of the kingdom (Luke 4:43). Jesus said the gospel of the kingdom will be preached to all nations (Matthew 24:14). After he rose from the dead, Jesus spoke to his disciples multiple times about the kingdom of God (Acts 1:3).

Throughout Acts, the apostles, and disciples, continued to preach about Jesus' kingdom realm. When Philip introduced Samaria to the good news of the kingdom, many were healed and delivered (Acts 8:12-13). In Athens, Paul spoke about God not being far from anyone (Acts 17:27), which is similar to Jesus' message about the kingdom being near. In Ephesus and Rome, Paul spoke about the kingdom and God did extraordinary miracles through him (Acts 19:8-11).

In Rome, Paul explained the kingdom of God to large numbers of people from morning until evening (Acts 28:23). Paul's kingdom message included speaking about Christ crucified (1 Corinthians 1:22-23) and his resurrection (1 Corinthians 15:1-5). Messianic prophecies include both a suffering servant (Isaiah 53:4-5) and a victorious king (Isaiah 11:1-5). Jesus is both the Lamb that was slain (Revelation 5:12) and the Chief Shepherd (1 Peter 5:4). The gospel message is about both Jesus' suffering and his kingship.

Jesus often described what it meant for him to be the king of the kingdom realm. Jesus said he was the Bread of Life (John 6:35), the Light of the World (John 8:12), the Gate for the Sheep (John 10:9), the Good Shepherd (John 10:11), the Resurrection and the Life (John 11:25), the Way, the Truth and the Life (John 14:6) and the True Vine (John 15:1).

God's dream is to reconcile the world to himself, in and through

Jesus. In and through Jesus, God revealed who he was, so that people could encounter him and be reconciled to him. When people encountered Jesus, they personally experienced the truth of the kingdom realm. They did not just hear theological truth.

It is easier to be reconciled to God when you have an experience of Jesus first and find out what he is like. Evangelism reveals king Jesus and his kingdom realm, so that people can discover how magnificent and awesome he is and choose to follow him.

Contrasting a 'conversion' and a 'kingdom' message

Some evangelism methods focus on describing the process of becoming a Christian. Whilst this is important, it is not where Jesus started. Jesus' message was about himself and his kingdom realm. The kingdom message is about who the King of Kings is, what he has done, what he is doing and our response to him. The invitation to enter the kingdom realm is more far-reaching than the invitation to be converted.

The 'sinner's prayer' is often used to lead someone in repentance[24]. The prayer typically includes statements like:
- I know that I am a sinner and ask for your forgiveness
- I believe you died for me and paid the price for my sin
- I repent and turn away from my sin
- I invite you into my life and receive you as saviour

Such a prayer, though Biblical, focuses on the problem, the solution, and the response we need to make. In other words, it focuses on conversion. Whilst conversion is an essential part of the gospel, it is only a part of the kingdom message. When we share the gospel, if we only share about conversion, we won't fully represent Jesus and his kingdom realm.

---

[24] en.wikipedia.org/wiki/Sinner's_prayer

It is worth noting that The Sinner's Prayer originated in the twentieth century, so has not been used for most of church history[25]. It is not a prayer that is found in the Bible, nor did Jesus or the apostles use the prayer. Though it can be helpful for some, it neglects several key biblical truths about Jesus' kingdom.

The table below illustrates the key differences in focus between conversion and kingdom messages. The contrast in the table is illustrating the difference in focus between the messages. It's not about what should be theologically included in a complete gospel description.

Conversion Message Focus	Kingdom Message Focus
You are a sinner	You don't yet know Jesus
You are condemned to hell	Your sin can be forgiven
Transactional – Jesus took your sin	Relational – you can be reconciled to God
God is distant	God is near
God's rejection of you and your sin	God accepts and wants to adopt you
Your problem of sin	Jesus is the solution to your sin
God's anger requires repentance	God's kindness leads you to repentance
Slavery to sin	Freedom from sin
Fixing your past problems and sin	Your future, new identity, and destiny
Disease caused by sin	Healing physically and emotionally
Getting saved	Entering the kingdom
Shame and guilt for sin	Forgiveness from sin
You will go to heaven when you die	You can bring heaven to earth now

---

[25] The Sinners Prayer: A Historical and Theological Analysis, by Paul Harrison Chitwood

Whilst what is shown under the conversion message may be true, it is not the only focus of Jesus' kingdom realm message. A conversion message typically focuses on what you are saved from, whereas the kingdom message focuses on what you are saved for, as well as what you are saved from.

Some evangelism methods can suggest that we first need to help people understand that they are sinners. This is not the approach Jesus used; he first introduced his kingdom realm. Experiencing Jesus, knowing what he is like and who he is, is the first step towards repentance.

Let's say we invited you to dinner to get to know you more. You arrived at our house and knocked on the front door. We opened the door and rather than greeting you and welcoming you in, we discussed the front door with you. We spoke about how strong the door was, how it kept people out of house that we did not want to enter. We showed you its multi-level deadlock system, its lever and mortice locks.

Sometimes we can present the gospel like this. We can focus on the 'door of sin' that separates us from God, rather than revealing Jesus 'the gate' (John 10:7) and 'the way' (John 14:6) to God so that people can get to know him, be saved and experience life to the full (John 10:9-10).

People's greatest need is to be *reconciled to God*. Repentance and forgiveness of sin opens the door to reconciliation and a relationship with God. A kingdom message reveals the Father, so people can experience his love and be reconciled to him. God's dream is to reconcile people to him, so they can relationally know him.

It is also worth comparing the message focuses in the table above with Greek and Hebrew thought perspectives. Western conversion methods are often based on Greek thought, which provide a logical approach to becoming a Christian. This can result in an intellectual ascent to the truth, rather than experiencing the truth.

Marvin R. Wilson says, "In Hebrew thought the essence of true godliness is tied primarily to a relationship, not a creed. The Lord is the God of Israel, and Israel is the people of God. Here is the leitmotif of biblical theology. The Torah gives direction to Israel on how to relate to the Creator, his people, and his world. Sin ruptures that relationship, but repentance brings forgiveness and restoration to fellowship." [26]

The kingdom message reveals the Father so we can be reconciled to him. It is primarily a relational message: "All things have been committed to me by my Father. No one knows who the Son is except the Father, and no one knows who the Father is except the Son and those to whom the Son chooses to reveal him." (Luke 10:22). Jesus showed the disciples what the Father was like (John 14:8).

Jesus says that Holy Spirit will prove the world to be wrong about sin because people do not believe in him (John 16:9). There is a link between being a sinner and not believing in Jesus, the king of the kingdom realm: "Whoever believes in him is not condemned, but whoever does not believe stands condemned already because they have not believed in the name of God's one and only Son." (John 3:18).

Holy Spirit is at work in unbelievers to help them believe in Jesus.

---

[26] Marvin R. Wilson, Our Father Abraham: Jewish Roots of the Christian Faith (1989), Page 138.

The kingdom gospel introduces people to the king, so that they can believe in him. Evangelism should lead to people believing in Jesus. If you don't believe in the king, then you can't enter his kingdom: Jesus said "If you do not believe that I am he, you will indeed die in your sins." (John 8:24).

Does awareness of being a sinner lead us to repentance? It may do, but the Bible says it is God's kindness that leads people to repentance: "Do you show contempt for the riches of his kindness, forbearance and patience, not realising that God's kindness is intended to lead you to repentance?" (Romans 2:4).

When Peter experienced Jesus' kindness at work through a miraculous catch of fish, he saw Jesus for who he was and then realised he was a sinful man: "When Simon Peter saw this, he fell at Jesus' knees and said, 'Go away from me, Lord; I am a sinful man!'" (Luke 5:8).

As people experience the king and his kingdom realm, they will find out what he is like, his character and how kind and good he is. The demonstration of his kindness, of signs, wonders and miracles will bring people to conviction (Romans 15:18-19). This will lead them to want to repent (turn from their sin and change their thinking and behaviour) and align their life to what is important to Jesus and his kingdom realm.

If we were to pray with someone to become a Christian, the focus would be wider than the traditional 'sinner's' prayer.' Such a prayer could include statements like[27]:

- I believe in you Jesus and accept your invitation to follow you for the rest of my life.

---

[27] This is an example prayer to illustrate a kingdom realm perspective on becoming a Christian. The prayer is not meant to provide a complete model for repentance or capture all theological aspects of the gospel.

- I choose to make our relationship the most important one in my life.
- Thank you for taking on yourself all that I did wrong so I could be forgiven and free.
- I give you all my failures, poor decisions, and mistakes in exchange for your new life.
- I forgive all those who have hurt me. Help me put it right with those who I have hurt or wronged.
- Show me what is important to you. Help me transform my thinking so I can think and live from your perspective.
- Teach me how to experience your love and how to love others.
- Please fill me with Holy Spirit so that I can know you, know who I am, be free and demonstrate your kingdom realm.
- I embrace the new life you are giving me and choose to hold nothing back from you.

Jesus used a kingdom message to bring people to himself. It is the approach used by Jesus and his apostles. It is how we should share the gospel, so that it transforms people's lives.

"Nightmares where there are body parts floating in the air."

We met Fred on an Alpha Course. Fred was an elderly gentleman who had served as a soldier during World War 2. He had many fascinating stories to tell and we so enjoyed hearing them. During the Alpha Course he started to encounter the kingdom realm. At night he would have visions where he would talk face-to-face with Jesus.

There was one war memory that continued to haunt him. During the D-Day[28] Campaign, he found himself in an impossible situation that had no easy choices. He was forced to give an order to kill

---

[28] en.wikipedia.org/wiki/Normandy_landings

captured enemy soldiers because they did not have enough food and water supplies to provide for all of them.

Since that time when he slept, he told us he had "nightmares where there are body parts floating in the air." When he became a Christian, Jesus met him in his pain and brought forgiveness and healing. Fred experienced salvation and Jesus' transforming kingdom realm; he has never had that nightmare again! Jesus freed him from the trauma of one of the most difficult experiences in his life.

"I had to choose to kill a soldier or see another family member killed."

We met Anna during an outreach into a housing estate in the town where we live. She was a 'larger than life' lady who was a community 'grandma' to many of the young mums who lived on the estate. She became a good friend and had a faith in Jesus.

She started to share her life story with us. She grew up in Eastern Europe and was part of a country's nobility. Her father opposed Stalin and they had to flee their home and travel across German-occupied countries to reach safety. Several of her family members were killed during their travels.

At this point in her life she was only a teenager but found herself in an impossible situation. She told us, "I had to choose to kill a soldier or see another family member killed." She chose to shoot and kill the soldier and save her sibling's life. Throughout her life she wondered whether God could ever forgive her for such an act. Anna then encountered the transforming kingdom realm as she experienced Jesus' forgiveness for one of the most traumatic experiences in her life. We had the joy of praying with her and seeing this burden lift from her life. Sadly, she died of cancer shortly after this, but she died knowing she was completely forgiven.

How can we describe the kingdom realm?

The sportswear company Nike's external brand "Just do it"[29] is hailed as one of the most successful brand images and marketing campaigns. In Greek mythology, Nike is the Winged Goddess of Victory[30].

The mythological associations for the brand Nike are flight, victory, and speed. Buying their product implies you can run faster and achieve victory. The brand appeals to your hopes, dreams and reasons for living rather than the product specifications.

Nike's *internal* company values[31] are different to their *external* brand. Their company values include "be a sponge", "evolve immediately" and "do the right thing" Nike use different language internally and externally. They use different language *internally* with their staff to the language they use *externally* with prospective customers.

What would happen if Nike mixed up its internal and external language in a marketing campaign? It would go something like this: here is our new range of sports trainers...evolve immediately and be a sponge! Using internal language in the wrong context may not effectively communicate the intended message and may even put off prospective customers from buying their products.

Yet we can do that when we share the gospel. We can take internal theological language that describes the gospel to Christians and use

---

[29] en.wikipedia.org/wiki/Just_Do_It
[30] en.wikipedia.org/wiki/Nike_(mythology)
[31] www.thebalancesmb.com/nike-mission-statement-and-maxims-4138115

it externally for evangelism. For example, Romans chapters 1 to 8 were written by Paul to the church in Rome, a Christian audience. This is an important distinction. He is writing theology to help and establish Christians in their salvation. He is not writing to unbelievers to help them understand the gospel.

Using Christian language and theology, which is often rooted in Jewish culture, is unlikely to connect with unchurched people in western culture. If you were speaking to a person without a religious background and said, "For all have sinned and fall short of the glory of God" (Romans 3:23), they may not understand what you are trying to say because the language and terminology is unfamiliar to them. Jewish culture has a framework for sin and righteousness, whereas modern western culture, for the most part, does not.

How much is the word 'sin' used in everyday life outside of a religious community? Rarely. The Greek origin for sin is failing to hit the mark[32], especially in spear throwing. The Hebrew originates in archery and literally refers to missing the centre of a target, i.e. error. Most people in Western society don't throw spears and few play archery! Even if they do, the word 'sin' is no longer commonly used in these activities.

So why would we use internal language externally, especially using words people may not be familiar with or know the meaning of? Jesus did not do this; he used stories and parables to explain his kingdom realm without using religious language. Jesus would often say,[33] "The kingdom is like …". He described the kingdom realm using cultural analogies and stories people could understand and relate to.

---

[32] hamartia, Strongs G266

[33] Many of Jesus' descriptions of the kingdom can be found in Matthew 13, Mark 4, and Luke 13.

Let us use an example of a sunset to explain the difference between internal and external language. Imagine a sunset over open sea; it looks spectacular. The changing rich colours in the sky are simply amazing. The reflection in the ocean is breathtaking. Watching the sun dip below the horizon is a perfect moment. Does this description create a desire in you to have such a moment and experience it first-hand?

What if we took a different approach and used science to explain the sunset? The colours of the sunset result from a phenomenon called scattering. Molecules and small particles in the atmosphere change the direction of light rays, causing them to scatter. Scattering affects the colour of light coming from the sky, but the details are determined by the wavelength of the light and the size of the particle.

Both descriptions of the sunset capture the moment but describe it differently. The internal language describes how it works scientifically, like theological language. The external language describes what it is like to experience it, like Nike's brand language. To unbelievers, Jesus described what his kingdom realm was like, so they could experience it.

Jesus describes his kingdom as a realm that is near and that has power to heal, raise the dead and drive out demons (Matthew 10:7-8). To enter his kingdom realm, Jesus says that we need to be born again (John 3:3). Moreover, he describes the arrival of his kingdom as the fulfilment of prophecy that will bring good news, freedom, healing, and favour (Isaiah 61:1-3).

In these and other Bible passages, Jesus describes what the kingdom realm is like when an unbeliever initially experiences it (such as healing and deliverance), how they can enter the kingdom realm (being born again) and what their life will look like once they are a Christian living in it (a bringer of good news and freedom to those around them, and transforming their city).

The term 'kingdom' it is not commonly used within western culture, so how can we explain it to unbelievers? The dictionary[34] defines a kingdom as a state or government having a king or queen as its head, anything conceived as constituting a realm or sphere of independent action or control and the spiritual sovereignty of God.

Incorporating these points, we can explain God's Kingdom using *external* language rather than *internal* theological terminology:

It is a realm where King Jesus has power over all sickness, death, hopelessness, poverty, despair, misfortune, mistakes, and failures. Within Jesus' realm, life prospers continually, it keeps growing, it has no limits or restrictions. His realm is inclusive, touching people of all ages, backgrounds, and nationalities. In his realm there is no hurt, pain, damage, or brokenness that can't be healed. This realm restores what has been lost or stolen. Jesus' realm is synonymous with the miraculous, where nothing is impossible.

People who enter his realm discover who they really are, why they were born, and what their destiny is. They fulfil their dreams. When they enter this realm, people encounter love and the Father from whom love originates. They are transformed into world changers by the Spirit permeating them with the Father's nature. They are given the ability to bring the wisdom and resources of heaven into their everyday lives. Their relationship to the King is clearly seen by the way they treat each other.

---

[34] www.thefreedictionary.com/kingdom

They reveal the kindness and nature of their King wherever they go. Their message is centred on love, freedom, grace, and forgiveness. It has the power to liberate people from any limitation from their upbringing, decisions, culture, or circumstances. They live with joy, peace, compassion, integrity, and courage. Their privilege is to partner with God in his dream to reconcile the world to himself.

Jesus personally invites you to be part of his realm. It is within everyone's reach, so why not reach out and experience it now?

Does this draw you in to want to experience Jesus' kingdom realm? The way we speak about the kingdom gospel can invite an encounter with Jesus. Our definition of the kingdom realm is not about a clever set of words to describe it. We chose these words to generate a hunger in unbelievers to experience Jesus and his kingdom realm.

What response to Jesus do you want to make after reading this description of the kingdom realm? When people discover and are touched by his kingdom realm, Jesus says that people will respond with joy and sell all they have to obtain it (Matthew 13:44-46). It is the greatest treasure anyone can have, there is no earthly treasure that can compare.

Whether people stumble over his kingdom realm or search for it, they celebrate, they experience joy, they value what they have found and give all they have in exchange for it. Jesus and his kingdom realm are literally 'out of this world' and worth giving everything for. Jesus can completely transform people's lives, whatever difficult circumstances they have faced.

The kingdom gospel also speaks about society transformation (Isaiah 61:4-6). This is part of the king's message. Once we are born again, Jesus has plans and a destiny for every one of us (Ephesians 2:10). The kingdom realm is not meant to be limited to an individual's salvation. That is just the starting point. The kingdom realm has the power to change people's lives, your community, your city, your nation, and even the world.

We often ask unbelievers if they want to experience the presence of God. We hold their hands and ask God to touch them. They experience happiness, peace, love, comfort, and miraculous healing. In these moments, unbelievers are experiencing Jesus' kingdom. Some unbelievers comment, "I have never felt anything like that before!"

A kingdom gospel that introduces the king and his kingdom realm will bring wonder, amazement, surrender and repentance. A message that only focuses on conversion and how to become a Christian may not.

How do we measure kingdom success?

It is important to understand how Jesus defines the success of his kingdom realm. Knowing this, we can learn to be successful and celebrate success when it happens. Success for the 'conversion message' is often seen as people praying the 'sinner's prayer', being born again and added to a church. Whilst this is important, the kingdom is broader than conversion so has a broader definition of success.

When Jesus was asked by John the Baptist's disciples whether he was the coming Messiah, he first demonstrated the kingdom realm's power through miraculous healing and afterwards gave his answer, "Go back and report to John what you have seen and heard: the blind receive sight, the lame walk, those who have leprosy are cleansed, the deaf hear, the dead are raised, and the good news is proclaimed to the poor." (Luke 7:22).

This is a very different definition of success to the conversion message. The definition of success for the kingdom message is people experiencing Jesus and his supernatural realm. When a believer shares with an unbeliever the kingdom realm and they hear and experience the good news, we celebrate success.

When we ran Alpha Courses, participating guests would often comment on how they felt peace or excitement whilst in the church building and when speaking to the Alpha Team. We would point out that they were feeling God's presence (Jesus' kingdom realm) and that they could, if they were a Christian, have that on the inside all the time, not just when they were with us on the course.

The success of the kingdom message is not limited to people becoming Christians, though of course that is a central part of it and something we greatly rejoice in. We found that introducing people to the kingdom realm during Alpha Courses led to an increase in the number of people we saw becoming Christians. Experiencing the kingdom was a key part of their salvation journey.

"Can you please pray for my wife's long-term back problem?"

We were flying to a European city for a weekend family break with our two youngest children. It was the first time they had both been on an aeroplane, and they were both very excited. After we landed, we got a taxi to the hotel where we would be staying. The taxi driver was very friendly and suggested various places we could visit during our stay.

As we arrived at the hotel Mark heard Holy Spirit say in his thoughts that the taxi driver had heart and circulation problems. When Mark shared what God has said to him, the taxi driver said this was true and that he periodically visits the doctors to check the condition and was due to go in a two days' time. God's timing is amazing. He knew the taxi driver's health was on his mind due to the forthcoming doctor's appointment!

The taxi driver was moved that God knew and cared about him. Before we got out of the taxi, we both put our hands on his shoulder and prayed that he would be completely healed. We thought that would be the last time we saw or heard from him.

Later that weekend the taxi driver rang our hotel and the receptionist put the call through to our room. We had just got back from a day out. Fiona picked up the phone and said to Mark the taxi driver who drove us from the airport wanted to speak to him. Mark was a little puzzled as to why that would be, but there was a thought in the back of his mind that this was an evangelistic moment.

Mark said hello and the taxi driver thanked him again for praying for him and then asked, "Can you please pray for my wife's long-term back problem?" So over the phone, Mark prayed with the taxi driver that God would miraculously heal his wife. After the call ended, we were both amazed and excited by how God works.

Activation

Reflect on these verses:

> *As you go, proclaim this message: "The kingdom of heaven has come near." Heal those who are ill, raise the dead, cleanse those who have leprosy, drive out demons. Freely you have received; freely give.*
> Matthew 10:7-8

Ask God:

- Am I experiencing the fullness of your kingdom realm in my own life?
- How can I best describe and demonstrate the kingdom realm, so people around me will want to experience it?
- Who do I know that is within reach of the kingdom realm?

Pray:

> *Father, thank you for your kingdom realm that I entered when I was born again. Help me understand its wonder, value and transformational power. Help me share the good news of the kingdom in a way that results in people giving their all to follow Jesus.*

To do:

- Write down what God said to you and meditate on it.
- This week, why don't you offer to pray for the person who God told you is close to the kingdom realm so they can encounter Jesus? After praying for them, ask if they felt something (e.g. peace, heat, physical pain leaving their body).

Further reading:

- Luke 4:14-21
- Matthew 13:44-46
- Luke 7:21-23

FOLLOW ME

It is the Holy Spirit's job to convict, God's job to judge, and my job to love.
(Billy Graham, Evangelist, Baptist Minister and Author)

"I became a Christian at the weekend."

Mark was due to start a new job, a year after graduating from University. Before he started, he prayed about his new job several times. On one occasion God gave him a picture of a wife praying for her unbelieving husband and said, "I want you to be part of answering her prayer." This was a new experience for Mark and he did not really know what to expect next.

On his first day of the new job, Mark joined a training course and sat next to a person called Stuart. Over the training course he and Mark got to know each other. During the course, there was a team exercise where each person had to draw a picture of an animal that represented him or her in some way, and then stand up in front of everyone to say why.

Mark was not sure what to draw, so he asked Holy Spirit for some help and an idea came to his mind. He drew a picture of a lion and said amongst other things, "I am a courageous person, because that was the way God made me." When Mark went back to his seat, Stuart's face lit up and said, "Are you a Christian? I have many questions about God" Over the next few weeks Stuart asked Mark lots of questions and mentioned that his wife was a Christian.

One Monday morning, a while later, Mark asked Stuart how his weekend went. Stuart replied, "I became a Christian at the weekend!" He went on to say that his wife was really pleased because she had been praying for him to become a Christian for some time. Prior to meeting Mark, Stuart had started his decision-making process to become a Christian. Through his wife's witness he was already aware of the reality of God and was interested in finding out more.

By answering his questions and sharing his testimony, Mark was able to help Stuart to go the next stage of becoming a Christian. Over the next few months, Stuart and Mark met frequently to discuss further what it meant to follow Jesus. Stuart now had more questions: he wanted to understand how to read the Bible, pray and change his life, because he now had this new relational connection with God.

This story taught Mark a lifelong lesson: to ask God for help when he needed it and to follow what God says in response, knowing that it is likely to open up an evangelistic moment.

Follower of Jesus

Many of us follow people on social media. We subscribe for the purposes of friendship, networking, entertainment, education, and business. We follow people to keep in touch, meet new people, learn new things, and grow our businesses. We do this because the people we follow will benefit and enrich our lives in some way.

The dictionary definition[35] for 'follow' include to go in the same direction, to do the same thing as someone else, to go or come after a person, to adhere to or practice, to go after in pursuit, to watch or observe closely, and to accept the guidance or leadership of a person.

Jesus' starting point with many people was to ask them to follow him. He personally invited many individuals with the phrase *"follow me."* The Bible also mentions when crowds followed Jesus. There are twenty-eight references in the Gospels about large crowds following him. He invited people from different parts of society to follow him, including Philip (John 1:43) and Levi (Luke 5:27-28).

Jesus said to his disciples, "Whoever wants to be my disciple must deny themselves and take up their cross and follow me." (Matthew 16:24) and "Whoever serves me must follow me; and where I am, my servant also will be. My Father will honour the one who serves me." (John 12:26). It is therefore not surprising that the Greek word Christianos means 'follower of Christ'[36].

So why did Jesus ask people to follow him? Jesus invited people to see what he and his kingdom are like before they decide to become a Christian. He wants people to see his heart of love, his trustworthy character, his unparalleled wisdom, and his supernatural power to change people's lives for the better.

Those of you with primary school children would know about 'show and tell' sessions where your child is asked to bring in an object of value from home and talk about it to the other children.

---

[35] www.thefreedictionary.com/follow
[36] Christianos, Strongs G5546

'Show and tell' sessions are also used in a business context and software development methodologies. The philosophy being that you demonstrate something and then talk about it.

Jesus employed a 'show and tell' approach to evangelism. He would 'show' the power of the kingdom realm and then 'tell' what the kingdom realm was like. It was rare for Jesus to talk about the kingdom without demonstrating it. Jesus' 'show and tell' happened wherever he went. His evangelism approach was to put his kingdom on display and look for people who wanted to follow him. There was no coercion, pleading, manipulation or fearful motivation of hell.

Jesus simply put the goodness, power, love, wisdom, and kindness of his Father on display. This often resulted in amazement and wonder: "All the people were amazed and said to each other, 'What words these are! With authority and power, he gives orders to impure spirits and they come out!' And the news about him spread throughout the surrounding area." (Luke 4:36-37). When the kingdom is put on display Jesus becomes known for his wisdom and power.

When the kingdom realm is put on display, people have a choice to follow Jesus or not. Seeing and experiencing the kingdom realm allows people to evaluate what Jesus is like, so they can make a choice to follow him or not. Not everyone will choose to follow Jesus. If they didn't, Jesus did not chase them down and ask them to reconsider. Even though Jesus loved the rich young ruler (Mark 10:21), he freely let him walk away after he rejected him, because he chose wealth instead.

Jesus also refused to water down his life-giving kingdom gospel to be more culturally or politically acceptable. When Jesus speaks about eating his flesh and drinking his blood, the disciples say, "This is a hard teaching. Who can accept it?'" (John 6: 60). Many disciples left him at this point, after which Jesus asked the Twelve, "You do not want to leave too, do you?" (John 6: 67).

Jesus gave the Twelve an opportunity to stop following him. Jesus did not use control and guilt to ensure they continued to follow him, but absolute freedom to walk away if they wanted. Peter replied, "Lord, to whom shall we go? You have the words of eternal life. We have come to believe and to know that you are the Holy One of God." (John 6:68).

Understanding the decision-making process

Becoming a Christian is a big decision. Making any big decision in our lives involves a process. Psychology regards decision-making[37] as "the cognitive process resulting in the selection of a belief or a course of action among several alternative possibilities. Every decision-making process produces a final choice, which may or may not prompt action. Decision-making is the process of identifying and choosing alternatives based on the values, preferences and beliefs of the decision-maker."

When people decide to become a Christian, it is not just a cognitive decision. We are constituted of body, mind, soul, and spirit. One or more of these can be involved in the decision-making process to become a Christian.

---

[37] en.wikipedia.org/wiki/Decision-making

For some, the logic of why they should be a Christian will be important. For others, experiencing God's perfect love will be a deciding factor. Those who experience a miraculous healing in their body may want to know the God that changed their life. Those without hope or lacking a sense of purpose may be drawn to a new beginning.

Father God woos[38] people into deciding to follow him: "No one can come to me unless the Father who sent me draws them, and I will raise them up at the last day." (John 6:44). Unbelievers are spiritually dead; being born again is supernatural, where our spirits are made alive in Christ (Ephesians 2:1-5). To become a Christian, people require Holy Spirit to work within them (John 1:12-13).

In the mid-nineties, we joined a short-term team in Hong Kong working with Jackie Pullinger[39], who preaches the gospel, reaches the poor and sees people set free from addictions. In her outreach meetings, drug addicts would come to the meetings still under the effects of heroin. During the meetings they would hear God speak to them, be born again, be baptised in the Holy Spirit and start speaking in tongues. All of this occurred while the drugs were still affecting their body.

Jackie introduced them to king Jesus and his kingdom realm. The drug addicts would experience salvation as they were born of the Spirit (John 3:5-6). It didn't seem to matter that they were on a drug 'high' as God was working in them regardless. When they 'sobered up' the following day, they knew something was different and wanted to follow Jesus.

---

[38] helkō, Strongs G1670 draws, impels, or leads
[39] www.ststephenssociety.com/en/aboutus

Introducing people to the kingdom realm is not an optional extra; it is an essential part of the decision-making process of becoming a Christian. Miracles prove the authenticity of Jesus and his kingdom. People become aware of the reality of God in a way they had not before (Acts 2:22).

In becoming a Christian, people tend to go through four stages:

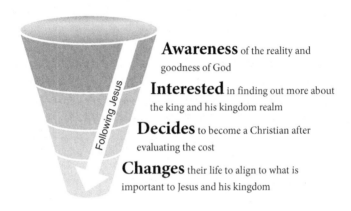

Awareness of the reality and goodness of God

Interested in finding out more about the king and his kingdom realm

Decides to become a Christian after evaluating the cost

Changes their life to align to what is important to Jesus and his kingdom

Through the 'show and tell' approach, unbelievers become *aware* of the reality of God, his love, compassion, wisdom, and power. This may be because of an answered prayer, miraculous healing, prophecy, or an encounter with his presence. People may need more than one supernatural experience before they show interest in finding out more.

After becoming aware of God, people may show an *interest* in finding out more. This is where we can introduce Jesus' invitation to follow him and invite them to more 'show and tell' kingdom realm opportunities. We may need to answer people's questions and objections, share God's heart of love with them or bring them healing. Whatever we do at this stage, it is important to further reveal the character of the Father, such as his kindness.

As the personal invitation from Jesus to follow him becomes more real, people will start evaluating whether they want to *decide* to become a Christian. During this stage we can ask Holy Spirit for revelation as to what is stopping them entering the kingdom. This could be the need to forgive people, repentance from a specific sin, hearing the voice of God, a more complete understanding of the gospel or an encounter with his amazing love and grace.

Once a decision has been made, people will want to know more about how to follow Jesus and *change* their life to align with what is important to him. The Bible calls this discipleship. New Christians will need to understand their new identity as children of God (1 John 3:1), water baptism (Romans 6:3-5), baptism in the Holy Spirit (Acts 19:1-7), and know how to live in freedom (Galatians 5:1). It is important we give people time to grow and not expect them to change overnight.

We can equip Christians and design evangelistic events, courses, and model a lifestyle to support each of the stages above. We can also adapt our church services for unbelievers to see, experience and learn about who Jesus is, what he is like and why he is worth following. The aim is to help people encounter God and understand what it means to follow Jesus, so they can make a well founded decision to become a Christian.

"I can barely hear it, it is like the faintest whisper."

Whilst out doing evangelism, Fiona met a woman, who was known to her through previous street outreach events. On this occasion she was talking with Fiona about lots of problems and difficulties that she had in her life.

Fiona asked Holy Spirit what was going on in her life and she felt Holy Spirit say the issues were linked to occult activity. Fiona very gently said to her, "Have you ever been to a medium, done tarot cards, or used a Ouija board? The woman replied, "No, I haven't done any of those before."

Fiona asked if she could pray for her. As Fiona was praying for the woman, one of the outreach team that was with Fiona heard Holy Spirit say that something had happened at a specific age during her teenage years. She shared this with the woman, saying, "God wants to heal you." The woman then said something very traumatic had happed to her at that age, at an isolated train station, but would not divulge any further details. Following this she said she never used trains again and would only use buses for public transport.

Fiona and the team member prayed for her to be healed from the traumatic event. Afterwards they asked the woman to see if God wanted to say anything to her. The woman listened for a few minutes and said, "I can barely hear it; it is like the faintest whisper." They encouraged her to listen again. The woman had a picture in her mind of two buses, one red and one black.

The woman said, "Jesus is telling me to get on the red bus, not the black bus. Fiona asked the woman "What do you think that means?" She replied, "Red is my favourite colour and Jesus is driving the red bus. He is asking me to get on the red bus. I am not to get on the black bus that represents black magic. That is what I used to be into for three years."

Fiona and the team member spoke about how Jesus was safe and that he is and always will be a safe person to drive the bus. They also talked to the woman about God wanting her to make a definitive decision to turn away from occult activity. They prayed for her that Jesus would break off any influence of black magic.

It's amazing how Jesus chose a bus in the woman's favourite colour, especially as the woman saw buses as a safe way to travel and always her preferred mode of transport! Through this picture of buses, Jesus was inviting the woman to follow him.

"My desire is to run a spiritual healing business from my new house."

During the first week of an Alpha Course, we were getting to know the guests over dinner. One lady started to speak passionately about a new business venture she was starting. She said, "My desire is to run a spiritual healing business from my new house." She wanted to be a Reiki[40] healer. What we did next caught out several Christians at the meal who had brought their unbelieving friends with them.

They expected us to point out it was wrong and that she shouldn't be doing that. We in fact just listened and took interest in her new venture, as it was important to her. The reason we took this approach was that we were confident Jesus himself would speak to her about it as she started to experience him during the course.

Jesus knew the best way and time to speak to her about it. As she began to experience the kingdom realm, over the following weeks she developed her own convictions it was wrong and when she became a Christian, she decided not to start that business. It is not our priority to correct people's morals, rather it is to help people encounter Jesus and for him to speak to them directly.

---

[40] en.wikipedia.org/wiki/Reiki

Reaching the decision point

It's important to realise that some people will follow Jesus for various reasons and not just because they want to believe in him. In Capernaum, some people followed Jesus because of his miracle of feeding the five thousand, "Very truly I tell you, you are looking for me, not because you saw the signs I performed but because you ate the loaves and had your fill." (John 6:26).

In Samaria there was a sorcerer named Simon, who followed the evangelist Philip and he was astonished by the great signs and miracles he saw. Even though Simon believed and was baptised in water, when he saw people baptised in the Spirit, he offered the Apostles money to have the same ability (Acts 8:13-19).

The Apostle Peter responded "May your money perish with you, because you thought you could buy the gift of God with money! You have no part or share in this ministry, because your heart is not right before God. Repent of this wickedness and pray to the Lord in the hope that he may forgive you for having such a thought in your heart. For I see that you are full of bitterness and captive to sin." (Acts 8:20-23).

Becoming a Christian requires making Jesus the most important thing in our lives, with a willingness to give up everything to follow him. Counting the cost involves evaluating whether there is anything in our lives that is more important than Jesus.

In the case of the rich young ruler, the love of money was stopping him entering the kingdom (Mark 10:17-23). Jesus loved him, but his love for money was preventing him from entering the kingdom. Note that for this individual, Jesus was focusing on the specific issue in his life that was stopping him from becoming a Christian, which will differ for others.

When people get married, the lifelong covenant vows include the promise to forsake all others for as long as they live. Before people get married, they first date and later get engaged. They do this to get to know each other. Most people do not rush into marriage until they know whether they can love someone and be faithful to them all their life.

When some people start dating, they may know quickly this is the one person they want to marry. For most people this is not the case and they will go through a process over months and years of getting to know what they are like, before they reach the point where they know they want to marry them.

Following Jesus allows people to see what he is like and decide based on love and commitment. Some will make this decision quickly and others may take a while. For example, When Jesus had told Nathanael he had seen him earlier under a fig tree, he responded quickly to Jesus (John 1:48-49). Whereas it took Peter a longer time of following Jesus before he understood who he really was (Matthew 16:16).

During the process of following Jesus, our goal for people is to repent, be reconciled to God and become a disciple. If people are enjoying experiencing the kingdom realm, but are not realising who Jesus really is, or their need to repent, we need to encourage them further on their journey. This can include getting them to listen to Jesus themselves as to what the next step is or what is holding them back.

Sometimes in our enthusiasm, we can tell people what we think the next steps are in them becoming a Christian. It is far better for people to hear from Jesus themselves, as after all, it is Jesus who they need to learn how to follow. The Samaritan woman who met Jesus at a well went back to her village and brought people to see Jesus themselves. They said to her, "We no longer believe just because of what you said; now we have heard for ourselves, and we know that this man really is the Saviour of the world." (John 4:42).

Sharing the gospel is primarily about introducing people to Jesus so that they can be reconciled to the Father. Remember God's dream? Repentance from sin and having faith are just part of that journey, not the outcome. The outcome is that they know Jesus and choose to follow him for the rest of their lives. This close and intimate relational connection with Jesus is foundational to them being a Christian so that they can follow him all their life, so let's start them on the right footing.

Evangelism should result in people encountering Jesus as they start to follow him. These experiences of Jesus will introduce them to the good news of the kingdom realm. They will personally experience Jesus' voice, love, goodness, healing, hope and life. When they find out who Jesus really is, the king of the kingdom realm, then repentance and faith will naturally follow. We shouldn't argue people into becoming a Christian. If we rely solely on using arguments as the basis for presenting Christianity it is not enough. To become a Christian, people need their own God-given conviction and experience of Jesus and his kingdom realm.

The outcome is not that they share our connection with Jesus, our experience, our church, or our denomination. Evangelism is not recruitment into our church. Jesus has a plan for everyone. Let him choose which people and church he wants him or her to connect with. It is Jesus' gospel, where he invites people to follow him.

In all aspects, Jesus is our perfect role model and our supreme example in soul winning. Jesus' 'show and tell' approach is an example to us all that he is looking for us to emulate. His 'show and tell' approach used parables to describe his kingdom realm and demonstrated its power to change lives. Within our daily lives we can regularly supernaturally demonstrate the love, power, kindness, and wisdom of the gospel of the kingdom.

"Can I take your wife home with me?"

Whilst on holiday, we were out for dinner at a restaurant. We got talking and building rapport with the people on the table next to us, an elderly lady and her middle-aged daughter. Fiona asked if they would recommend anything from the menu, as they had eaten in the restaurant before.

Fiona had noticed the elderly lady was in a wheelchair and, about halfway through the meal, Fiona asked her how long she had been in the wheelchair. Her daughter replied, "Two weeks! On the day we arrived my mother tripped over in the bathroom and twisted her ankle. I have been pushing her around for our entire holiday."

The elderly lady had not been able to walk on it, it was painful, swollen and had been keeping her awake at night. They had been to a doctor to get an x-ray to check the ankle was not broken. Her lack of mobility had impacted her, and her daughters' holiday and they were going home the following day, because the holiday was coming to an end.

Fiona asked if she could pray for the elderly lady and she enthusiastically said yes. Fiona asked if she could put her hand on the lady's ankle and quietly prayed a simple prayer that all the pain would go, and it would be completely restored and healed in Jesus' name. After talking some more, we finished our meals and said goodbye.

The next morning, we saw the elderly lady and her daughter near the holiday accommodation reception. We went over, greeted them, and asked how they were. The elderly lady replied, "I had the best night's sleep of the holiday, my ankle feels so much better." We saw that the swelling in her ankle had visibly reduced considerably.

The elderly lady then jokingly said to Mark, "Can I take your wife home with me, she is lovely!" We laughed and politely declined, saying it was lovely to meet them and we would continue to pray for them. We can take everyday moments, such as eating in a restaurant, to bring the kingdom realm.

Activation

Reflect on this verse:

> *"No one can come to me unless the Father who sent me draws them, and I will raise them up at the last day."*
> John 6:44

Ask God:

- How can I invite people to follow you, Jesus, so they can find out what you are like?
- How can I share the gospel in a way that helps unbelievers make a good decision to follow you?
- How can I help unbelievers hear your voice and personally experience you?

Pray:

> *Father, thank you for coming to seek and save the lost. Help me to introduce people to you, so they can experience your love and hear your voice. Help me see the evangelistic moments that you want to invite me into.*

To do:

- Write down what God said to you and meditate on it.
- This week, why not offer to pray for someone who is not a Christian and ask him or her to listen to Jesus, to see what he wants to say to him or her?

Further reading:

- John 6:44-47
- Luke 4:36-37
- Acts 8:9-25

LOVING PEOPLE

It's not complicated. Just love the one in front of you.
(Heidi Baker, Missionary and Author)

"I do feel calmer."

Fiona was leading an outreach team within a local town centre and there were several fun outreach activities going on. A man walked by and started to be verbally abusive, shouting things like, "Why do you believe in all this rubbish? You people are so deluded! You people should be ashamed of yourself, asking people for money and exploiting people!" He was very angry and agitated.

Fiona thought that it was not okay for this man to shout at her team and wondered what he was angry about, because she guessed that the team was not the real issue. She decided to approach the man and asked him his name, he replied "Tony." Fiona said, "You seem really angry Tony, what is the matter?" Tony then reiterated all the things he had been shouting, along with a few choice expletives.

Fiona asked Tony if she could hold his hands, he replied, "Yeah, whatever." Fiona said, "You look like you need some peace, would you like some peace? I have plenty of it and you can have some of mine." At this point Tony looked a bit confused and was still ranting about on about taking money. Fiona said, "We are not taking any money here today. Everything we are doing today is free; we want to bless people and do them good. We are putting activities on for children, we are loving our community."

Tony softened a little and he walked off. Over the next hour, he was approached twice by different members of the evangelism team using 'clues' that God had spoken to them prior to the outreach. God often gives us 'clues' so we can find the people he wants to touch during the outreach. We put the 'clues' into categories on what we call a treasure map, as the people we want to find who match the 'clues' are 'God's treasure'. The categories we use are location, appearance, names, dates, and needs. This supernatural evangelism method is called Treasure Hunting[41].

Tony then came back to where Fiona was in the town centre and she approached him again to ask how he was doing. Tony apologised and said he shouldn't have been so aggressive. He again then mentioned taking money. Fiona then said, "Just because there are some bad apples, don't tar us all with the same brush." Fiona wondered whether he had had a bad experience of a religious group asking for money.

Tony then said to Fiona, "I do feel calmer." Fiona replied, "That's because you received some peace, Jesus' peace, that is why you feel calmer." Tony apologised again and said he was 'out of order'. When Tony received peace, he had a tangible experience of God; this may have been Tony's first real experience of Jesus and his kingdom. It was also helpful to undo negative stereotypes about Christians. Sometimes in our evangelism we need to make amends for unhelpful things that some Christians may have said or done in the past.

---

[41] Kevin Dedmon, The Ultimate Treasure Hunt: A Guide to Supernatural Evangelism Through Supernatural Encounters (2013).

Tailor made gospel

When we buy clothes, we can buy either ready-to-wear, mass-produced standardised size clothes or bespoke/haute couture made-to-measure clothing, which is made using higher quality material and techniques so the garment will perfectly fit us.

We also get a similar choice during evangelistic moments. We can use standard pre-packaged gospel messages, or we can share the gospel in a way that is tailored to the unique person who we are speaking with. If we are to follow Jesus' example, we find that he tailored his message to the uniqueness of the person he was speaking with. The apostles and disciples did the same, adapting their message to the culture they were in.

Jesus used everyday stories to describe the kingdom realm. He called them parables. Jesus would often say, "The kingdom of God is like…" using an everyday cultural scenario to describe the kingdom realm and how it works. Jesus did not use pre-packaged messages. Rather he uniquely shared the kingdom realm with the person or people he was with.

A Brilliant[42] is a diamond or other gemstone cut in a form with numerous facets to have exceptional brilliance. Think of the kingdom realm in this way. When we meet someone, we can ask Holy Spirit which facet of the kingdom realm to share with them. People may need to encounter different aspects of Jesus' character, depending on where they are in their journey of following him. They may need to encounter Jesus as love, hope, wisdom, kindness, mercy, provision, or healer before they are ready to receive him as Saviour and Lord.

---

[42] en.wikipedia.org/wiki/Brilliant_(diamond_cut)

Individuals have been shaped by their history and life experience, which includes their culture and upbringing. This will affect how they think, speak and act. We want to explain how the gospel message is relevant to an individual, using language they will understand. Choosing the right stories and analogies is important, as we want to profoundly impact them with the reality of the kingdom realm.

God has chosen the time in history when each person would be born, including which culture they would be born into. "God did this so that they would seek him and perhaps reach out for him and find him, though he is not far from any one of us." (Acts 17:27). When we meet someone, God wants to speak to him or her in a way they will understand. The kingdom realm transcends all cultures and can personally impact individuals.

When we were working with Jackie Pullinger in Hong Kong, we saw amazing healings and people miraculously freed from drug addiction. It had a profound effect on us, even to this day. During one of her outreach meetings Jackie referenced, "I am the bread of life" (John 6:35), but she actually said, "I am the rice of life." In a culture where rice is eaten daily (and bread hardly ever), Jackie was adapting her message to be relevant to the culture she was in.

Paul had the same approach. Although he was free, he chose to identify with those he was with, to win as many as possible to the gospel. He says, "I have become all things to all people so that by all possible means I might save some. I do all this for the sake of the gospel, that I may share in its blessings." (1 Corinthians 9:22-23). Paul understood the value and importance of sharing the kingdom realm in a culturally relevant way.

The culture we are born into and grow up in profoundly affects how we see the world and what we consider normal. Culture influences our learning, behaviour, thinking, values, attitudes, clothing, food, language, literature, politics, philosophy, and art. Culture is the lens through which our world is both shaped and interpreted.

For example, cultures differ in how they evaluate truth. Greeks primarily process truths in the abstract; Hebrews primarily process truths in the concrete[43]. Therefore, Greeks tend to value ideas and knowledge, whereas Hebrews tend to value character and tangible expressions and experiences in life. It is important to realise that neither is superior, but our cultural viewpoint would value one above the other.

We were once given this example. An elderly person from an Eastern Culture is informed that 'coffee does not grow in cold climates' and 'England has a cold climate', and then asked whether coffee can grow in England. Some would answer 'I don't know, I have never been to England'. For the older Eastern generations *experiencing* something is part of the process of evaluating truth.

Movies are often adapted for different cultures[44]. In Pixar's film *Inside Out*, different culturally relevant vegetables were used. The main character Riley refused to eat broccoli in the American version, but in the Japanese version Riley refuses to eat green bell peppers. In the film *Captain America: The Winter Soldier*, the character Steve Rogers creates a to-do list in the early part of the film. Marvel Studios created ten versions of the to-do lists for different cultural audiences around the world.

---

[43] For more on this subject refer to Part III of Our Father Abraham: Jewish Roots of the Christian Faith by Marvin R. Wilson (1989).
[44] mentalfloss.com/article/67638/9-movies-were-changed-international-audiences

In Hong Kong meat is often served on the bone in bite sized chunks. The cultural norm is to take the meat off the bone inside your mouth, without using your fingers and then spit the bone out on the table. It is considered rude to put fingers in your mouth but not to spit a bone on the table! Western culture regards it as somewhat different; it would be rude to spit a bone on the table! Our culture teaches us to value what is right and wrong, even if we don't perceive that some 'rights and wrongs' are relative between cultures and not absolute.

When we share the gospel with people, they will interpret what we say and do through their cultural lenses. The language we use can either be a help or a hindrance. We can learn to tailor the gospel message and share it in way that considers a person's culture and uniqueness. This does not mean we change what the gospel means, rather it means we share it in a way that will be meaningful.

Jesus and the apostles preached cultural messages

In the early chapters of Acts, the audience was primarily Jewish. Peter brought context, meaning and explanation to Jesus' life, death, resurrection, and ascension[45]. Through culturally relevant messages, drawing on fulfilment of Old Testament prophecies, he powerfully presented Jesus as the Messiah and the gift of the Holy Spirit being available to all.

Old Testament references would have been important to the Jews, as that is how they would evaluate what Jesus said and did. They would have grown up learning and reciting the Old Testament; it was familiar and well known to them.

---

[45] Examples of messages to Jews include Acts 2:14-41, Acts 3:11-24, and Acts 4:8-12.

Jesus also referenced the Ten Commandments, when speaking to the Jewish rich young ruler, which was his cultural framework for understanding God (Mark 10:17-19).

Paul's evangelistic messages in Athens drew on their local cultural objects of worship, not the Old Testament (Acts 17:22-23). When the evangelist Philip spoke with the Ethiopian eunuch (Acts 8:26-40), he explained the meaning of Isaiah 53. Isaiah's prophecy was describing the death of Jesus from a Jewish perspective, using cultural worship practices. The eunuch needed someone to explain it to him in a way he could understand. Note that Philip does not use a pre-packaged gospel message, but rather explains the gospel starting with the Old Testament passage the eunuch was reading.

Consider the objects of worship that are in your culture that could help share the gospel in a relevant way. Art and media often tell stories about our own cultural values, heroes, successes, and failure. Films and novels provide opportunities to describe the gospel using cultural language that does not include religious jargon. No analogy will be perfect but can still be used in a powerful way to influence people in their thinking about Jesus and his kingdom realm.

We can quote the Bible directly in evangelistic moments, but we could also quote a familiar cultural reference that illustrates a truth in the Bible. Cultural references from films, TV programmes, poetry or songs can be used to tell someone the good news of Jesus and his kingdom in a cultural language they may more easily understand. Jesus often told cultural stories to the Jews to illustrate the kingdom realm, without directly quoting the Old Testament.

In every culture God puts kingdom realm truths that can create openings and opportunities to connect people with Jesus. Every culture has things that are open, neutral, or hostile to the gospel. If we listen, Holy Spirit will reveal to us the openings in our culture that will help us preach and demonstrate the kingdom realm.

At an Easter guest service, Mark preached an evangelistic message using three well-known people in Western culture that he used as archetypes of Jesus:

- Nelson Mandela[46], who was once described by Rev. Jesse Jackson[47] as a 'suffering servant'. He believed in a better world where there was freedom from apartheid and racism. Nelson Mandela was willing to suffer to bring about this freedom.

- Edith Cavell[48], a British nurse in the First World War who became a 'saviour' of two hundred soldiers she helped to escape, even though it cost her life when she was sentenced to death for treason.

- Ashton Kutcher[49], an actor and investor, who has become a 'redeemer' through his anti-human trafficking organisation Thorn,[50] rescuing thousands of victims.

Drawing on these three modern-day examples enabled an introduction of Jesus as a suffering servant, saviour, and redeemer for the entire human race. Using these people's stories helped to explain Biblical references to the cross and resurrection. It is important to describe the gospel in a culturally meaningful way, using language that people will understand.

---

[46] en.wikipedia.org/wiki/Nelson_Mandela

[47] en.wikipedia.org/wiki/Jesse_Jackson

[48] en.wikipedia.org/wiki/Edith_Cavell

[49] en.wikipedia.org/wiki/Ashton_Kutcher

[50] www.wearethorn.org

We can use terminology in our evangelism that is not culturally relevant to those that have not had a Church or Sunday school background. Terms such as 'accepting Jesus', 'repentance', 'surrender to Christ', 'make Jesus Lord of your life' are not culturally common phrases and are not necessarily helpful in enabling people to understand the gospel.

Here are some alternative common cultural words and phrases that can be used to describe Biblical terms:

Term	Biblical Meaning	Alternative Words
Sin	fault, error, offence against God, to miss the mark	failure, wrongdoing, wanting to live life without God
Lord	supreme authority, master, sovereign, title	leader, royalty, king, ruler
Atonement	appease, conciliate, expiate, merciful	sacrifice, substitute, pay debt, redeem
Saviour	deliverer, preserver	hero, liberator, restorer, freedom
Repent	change one's mind, sorrow, obtain God's pardon	paradigm shift, think and live differently

Not all of these words and phrases may fully represent every aspect of the Biblical terms, but they will help to communicate the gospel in a culturally relevant way. If we share the gospel using culturally relevant language and meaning, it is likely to have a more successful outcome.

The kingdom can be countercultural

Another important factor about culture is that the kingdom realm will, in places, be counter-culture to our own culture. Jesus often told cultural stories that ended differently than expected to demonstrate that the kingdom realm was counter-cultural. In the parable of the lost son (Luke 15:11-31), when the father saw him, he was filled with compassion and ran to his son, threw his arms around him and kissed him.

This is counter-culture to the then Jewish culture because the son's behaviour would have deserved death (Deuteronomy 21:18-21). Also, an older father running to meet and forgive his son was not the cultural norm. Through this story Jesus was able to reveal the Father heart of God and challenge the cultural expectation that punishment was the appropriate course of action.

When we ask people to become Christians, we are not just expecting them to stop their 'obvious' sin, but also start leading a life that aligns with God's kingdom realm, which at times will be counter-cultural. For example, Paul and Peter were counter-cultural. Even though they were Jewish by birth, they ate with Gentile believers in Antioch (Galatians 2:11-13).

Western culture has some great values including personal freedom, tolerance, and the rule of law. We also have many cultural norms such as respect and fairness. In the UK we also have queuing and regularly talking about the changing weather!

The kingdom realm is counter-culture to western culture in several areas. For example, western culture values diversity and inclusion, but Jesus is the only way to God rather than all faiths leading to

God (Acts 4:12). Western culture is also very sexually permissive, but as Christians we will avoid sexual immorality (1 Thessalonians 4:3-8).

With the kingdom realm we encourage and celebrate each other (1 Thessalonians 5:11), whereas western culture often puts people down and can be cynical. Kingdom culture is generous (Luke 6:38), whereas western culture tends to gain wealth mostly for personal benefit.

Sharing the gospel in a culturally relevant way to help people encounter Jesus and his kingdom is key, but it must not exclude explaining the necessity of repentance, especially where it is counter-cultural.

People are unique

Snowflakes are unique, as no two are perfectly identical due to the estimated 10^{19} (10 quintillion) water molecules that make up a typical snowflake. At a distance snowflakes look the same, but under a microscope they are different. People can look similar or even the same at a distance, but God has made each person unique. A person's combination of the way they look, personality, genetics, gifts, and abilities make them unique.

Jesus affirmed the importance of rescuing an individual in the parable of the lost sheep: "I tell you that in the same way there will be more rejoicing in heaven over one sinner who repents than over ninety-nine righteous people who do not need to repent." (Luke 15:7).

If every person is unique, a pre-packaged, 'one-size fits all' gospel message may not be the best approach. It would be better to partner with Holy Spirit to tailor a message that perfectly fits someone. As every individual is God's design, Holy Spirit will know how to speak to him or her in a way that will take him or her further forward on their journey to salvation. People we meet will already have Holy Spirit working in their lives.

During evangelistic moments, God wants to speak deeply to an individual to communicate that he knows them, wants to heal them and do them good. He knows about each person and can therefore speak profoundly to individuals about them and their lives. We can make time to listen to Holy Spirit and stop for a few moments and share the kingdom realm with someone.

People have life dreams and failures, hopes and disappointments, strengths and weaknesses, confidence and uncertainty, plans and questions, joy and pain. Holy Spirit will know conversations they recently had and their own private thoughts. Holy Spirit can reveal to us hidden pain, unfulfilled dreams, financial difficulties, relationship issues, healing needs, and poor self-image. The information that Holy Spirit reveals can often lead individuals to the God who knows and cares about them.

"Do you know what God thinks of you?"

Mark was buying some food in a supermarket. As he unloaded the food onto the conveyor belt, he started to build rapport with the shop assistant. Mark suddenly felt the presence of God and realised he was being invited into an evangelistic moment. Holy Spirit then said to Mark that the shop assistant was doing well in her life, making good decisions for those around her.

Mark asked her, "Do you know what God thinks of you?" He then shared with her that God thought she was doing well. Mark asked whether she herself shared God's opinion of her. She said she did not think she was doing well but began to smile as she heard God's opinion. Mark encouraged her not to be hard on herself, which is a common western cultural practice, as God loved her and thought well of her.

"No-one has ever told me that before."

Fiona was away for a weekend as she was speaking at a woman's conference. She popped into a newsagent to buy some refreshments. As she began to speak with the shop assistant, Holy Spirit gave her a specific date. The date appeared quickly in her thoughts so she knew this was likely to be from God.

She asked the shop assistant whether the date meant anything to her. It was very close to the shop assistant's birthday! Fiona was encouraged and the shop assistant was intrigued. Fiona than shared with her that she was loved by God and valued by him.

The shop assistant was impacted by this and exclaimed, "No-one has ever told me that before." Communicating that every single human being is known and loved by God is an important part of the kingdom gospel message. In western culture, many people struggle to find their identity and know they are loved and valued.

Activation

Reflect on these verses:

> *Though I am free and belong to no one, I have made myself
> a slave to everyone, to win as many as possible. To the Jews I
> became like a Jew, to win the Jews. To those under the law I
> became like one under the law (though I myself am not under
> the law), so as to win those under the law. To those not having
> the law I became like one not having the law (though I am not
> free from God's law but am under Christ's law), so as to win
> those not having the law. To the weak I became weak, to win
> the weak. I have become all things to all people so that by all
> possible means I might save some. I do all this for the sake of
> the gospel, that I may share in its blessings.*
> 1 Corinthians 9:19-23

Ask God:

- What are the objects of worship in my culture that can help me to share the good news of the kingdom?
- What culturally relevant stories do I know that will help explain the kingdom realm?
- How can I share you Jesus and your kingdom realm without using religious jargon?

Pray:

> *Father, thank you for choosing the time and culture that
> I have been born into so that I could reach out and find
> you. Help me to share the kingdom realm in a way that is
> relevant to those I meet. Help me to hear your voice clearly
> for the unique individuals that I will meet in the evangelistic
> moments you will invite me into.*

To do:

- Write down what God said to you and meditate on it.
- This week, whilst you are with someone who is not a Christian, try sharing something about Jesus and his kingdom realm using a cultural story.

Further reading:

- Mark 10:17-31
- Luke 15:1-10
- Acts 17:22-34

GOD'S DREAM

BEING SUPERNATURAL

*The Gospel is 'Good News', not 'Good History', because
when it's preached, it happens.*
(Reinhard Bonnke, Evangelist and Author)

"You have got to be kidding!"

We had landed in America for a family holiday after a twelve-hour flight. We picked up our hire car and drove two hours to our hotel. Even though we were excited to be on holiday, we were tired, jet lagged, and looking forward to getting some sleep.

As we checked in to the hotel, God spoke to Mark about the receptionist having pain in his back and shoulder. Mark's initial reaction to God's invitation to partner with him was, "You have got be kidding! Why now? I just want to sleep, don't you know God how I feel right now?"

After recognising and processing his feelings and thoughts, Mark felt God's compassion for the receptionist. When God shares his heart for a person near us, it may not feel convenient. In these moments it is important not to condemn ourselves if we don't immediately feel like taking part, as we will not always have evangelism at the forefront of our mind.

When God invites us into an evangelistic moment, he knows we can make the most of the moment, regardless of how what we are feeling and thinking. There is grace and strength for the moment as the gospel gives us a readiness to share it at any time (Ephesians 6:15). Mark asked the receptionist if he had pain in his shoulder and lower back. The receptionist thought Mark was describing his own pain and offered to find him some painkillers. Mark thought to himself, "This evangelistic moment is not going well!"

He replied to the receptionist saying he himself had no pain but wondered whether they did. The receptionist said yes and asked how he knew. Mark explained that God had spoken to him and that he cared for the receptionist and wanted to heal him. Mark then asked if he could pray for healing. The receptionist said yes, but asked if Mark could come back later when he was less busy.

We went to our rooms, unpacked, and settled the children into bed. Fiona then prayed for Mark and he went off to find the receptionist. As Mark reached the hotel entrance it was less busy, so Mark asked the receptionist whether this was a good time to pray. The receptionist agreed and asked Mark to come with him to the business suite, so they could talk in private.

Mark spoke to the receptionist about the goodness of God and asked if he could put his hand on his shoulder to pray. The receptionist agreed and Mark prayed a short prayer, asking God to heal his shoulder and back. Mark then headed back to the hotel room for some much-needed sleep!

Two days later after a day of sightseeing, as we came into the hotel, we saw the receptionist. Mark asked how he was. He said, "The pain has completely gone!" The receptionist then acknowledged that he had been worried about the pain and thought it was a serious issue and had been scared to visit the doctor. Mark encouraged the receptionist that it was God who healed him, because he cared for him. Mark also suggested he try speaking to God himself and to read the Bible to find out more about Jesus.

Jesus' supernatural kingdom

Jesus is *the evangelist* and the supreme example to us of how to do evangelism supernaturally. Jesus came to seek and save those who are lost. We can learn from how he did evangelism, such as his conversation with the woman at the well in Samaria. Jesus was hot and tired from the journey and sat down by Jacob's well.

When a Samaritan woman came to draw water from the well, Jesus asked her for a drink. She was initially surprised because Jesus, a Jew, culturally did not speak with Samaritans. Jesus then replied, "If you knew the gift of God and who it is that asks you for a drink, you would have asked him and he would have given you living water." (John 4:10).

After a discussion about 'living water' Jesus asked her to get her husband. She replied saying she has no husband, after which Jesus said, "You are right when you say you have no husband. The fact is, you have had five husbands, and the man you now have is not your husband. What you have just said is quite true" (John 4:17-18).

The woman thought that Jesus must be a prophet and asks him a theological question about where geographically to worship. Jesus replied, "A time is coming and has now come when the true worshippers will worship the Father in the Spirit and in truth, for they are the kind of worshippers the Father seeks. God is spirit, and his worshippers must worship in the Spirit and in truth." (John 4:23-24). Jesus then finished the conversation by telling her he was the Messiah.

This story is profound for many reasons, but chiefly because this woman is one of the first people to whom Jesus reveals his identity as the Messiah. This woman is not one of his disciples, was not culturally allowed to have contact with Jews and was not righteous. Yet none of these issues were a barrier to Jesus telling her he was the person she was waiting for – the Messiah.

Let's follow Jesus' approach through this story. Firstly, Jesus uses an everyday cultural moment to begin a conversation and introduce spirituality. In our western culture, think about Jesus at a coffee shop! Despite her cultural complaint about Jews and Samaritans, Jesus starts his journey by introducing the concept of 'living water' while they are next to a well. Jesus is using an analogy and relevant visual aid to describe the kingdom realm, rather than theological language.

Secondly, Jesus knows personal information about her. Note how Jesus uses this information: he speaks with grace and gentleness. At no point does he label her a 'sinner' or 'adulterer', he does not condemn her. Jesus also does not just blurt out everything he heard in one go. Rather he takes her on a journey of self-realisation by asking a question. He does not at any point preach at her; it is entirely a conversation between them both.

Thirdly, Jesus gives time to answer her questions. As Jesus knew about her five husbands, she realises that Jesus is somebody out of the ordinary and somehow connected to God. She then uses this moment to ask Jesus her most important theological questions. Jesus takes time to answer them, knowing that answering them is important to her journey to faith.

Fourthly, Jesus shares his perspective with her about worship. Jesus speaks to her about a Father who is seeking worshippers; he is revealing something about the Father's nature to her. Maybe the reason she has had five husbands is because her father was either dead, absent or did not seek her out to spend time with her. We can't know for sure, but maybe Jesus is speaking into her relational brokenness and her need of a father.

Fifthly, Jesus reveals himself as the Messiah. This is is important in any evangelism, that we introduce people to the king and his kingdom realm, so that they discover how amazing he is and choose to follow him. The result of this supernatural conversation is that she goes back to her village, invites others to meet Jesus, leading to many more Samaritans becoming believers (John 4:39-42).

Brian McLaren[51], pastor and author, sums up Jesus' approach like this: "Jesus was short on sermons, long on conversations; short on answers, long on questions; short on abstraction and propositions, long on stories and parables; short on telling you what to think, long on challenging you to think for yourself."

Jesus uses the same approach with others. When he first meets Zacchaeus, despite being a tax collector, Jesus doesn't make a point of highlighting his dishonest, corrupt lifestyle of exploiting people. He treats him with value and dignity by going to his house for a meal, explains the kingdom and finds him ready for repentance and salvation (Luke 19:5-9).

---

[51] en.wikipedia.org/wiki/Brian_McLaren

Baptism in the Spirit

There are many Biblical reasons why we are baptised in the Spirit, including: speaking in tongues (Acts 2:4), ability to prophesy (Acts 19:6), character (Galatians 5:22), inner strength (Ephesians 3:16) and experiencing God's love (Romans 5:5). Another reason is that it enables us to carry out the Great Commission.

Jesus describes his kingly mission as: "The Spirit of the Lord is on me, because he has anointed me to proclaim good news to the poor. He has sent me to proclaim freedom for the prisoners and recovery of sight for the blind, to set the oppressed free, to proclaim the year of the Lord's favour." (Luke 4:18-19). Jesus gives us the same mission: "'As the Father has sent me, I am sending you.' And with that he breathed on them and said, 'Receive the Holy Spirit.'" (John 20:21-22).

Joel's prophecy provides a link between baptism in the Spirit and the harvest: "And afterwards, I will pour out my Spirit on all people. Your sons and daughters will prophesy, your old men will dream dreams, your young men will see visions. Even on my servants, both men and women, I will pour out my Spirit in those days. And everyone who calls on the name of the Lord will be saved." (Joel 2:28, 29 and 32).

God's promised outpouring of the Spirit includes the promise that "everyone who calls on the name of the Lord will be saved." When the Spirit was poured out at Pentecost, they experienced a violent wind, tongues of fire and spoke in other languages. As a direct result of this, many people were saved.

Our evangelism is meant to be empowered by the Holy Spirit. The

Holy Spirit gives us the words to say, boldness, wisdom, power to heal the sick and enables us to bring in the harvest. Evangelism without the Holy Spirit can often be something of an uphill struggle.

It is not designed to work without the empowering of the Holy Spirit. We are meant to preach the gospel by the Holy Spirit (1 Peter 1:12). When we receive the Holy Spirit, we undergo a stunning transformation – Jesus shares with us his heart, ability, authority, and power. As Christians, baptism in the Holy Spirit should lead to people being saved around us.

Following the baptism of the Spirit at Pentecost, three thousand people were saved in a day (Acts 2:41), people were then saved daily and added to the church (Acts 2:47), resulting in the Jerusalem church growing to over five thousand men (Acts 4:4). This was normal in the first century church. Their baptism in the Spirit resulted in harvest. Their experience of the Holy Spirit included prophecy, visions, tongues, miraculous healing, but also salvation on a large scale.

The Jewish Feast of Pentecost is a harvest festival, celebrating the first fruits (Exodus 23:16). When the Holy Spirit was poured out at Pentecost, this was the first fruit of God's salvation harvest. It was experienced by people from every nation (Acts 2:5). This was just the beginning. Jesus tells us that the harvest is ready and there is a need for harvesters (Luke 10:2).

Throughout Acts, evangelism is inherently supernatural and is often initiated supernaturally by God. When the gospel first came to the Gentiles (Acts 10:1-48), an angel visited Cornelius, Peter had a vision and the Holy Spirit came on the Gentiles during his message. When the first recorded Ethiopian became a Christian (Acts 8:26-40), Philip received direction from an angel and the

Holy Spirit, and at the end of the story he supernaturally teleports to another town!

When we engage with the Holy Spirit, evangelism is different. Whether we receive prophetic revelation, see a miraculous healing, or pray for an unbeliever to experience the presence of God, our evangelism goes up a level. This is how God has designed evangelism to be, it was never meant to be just words and clever sounding arguments. We are empowered to bring in the harvest.

Supernatural miracles

Western culture places a high value on explaining how things work and logical thinking. Western culture can influence us to explain the gospel without leading people to experience it. Jesus offered both. He asked people to follow him, so he could show them his kingdom realm so that they might end up choosing him as their king.

Jesus didn't differentiate between talking about the kingdom and demonstrating it. At a house in Capernaum, Jesus spoke to large crowds and healed a paralysed man. The friends of the paralysed man lowered him through the roof, so he was within reach of Jesus. Jesus forgave his sin and healed him: "He got up, took his mat and walked out in full view of them all. This amazed everyone and they praised God, saying, 'We have never seen anything like this!" (Mark 2:12).

In this story we see multiple aspects of the kingdom realm. We see the forgiveness of sin, miraculous healing, Jesus revealing that he is God, and people's amazement. This is the way the gospel of the kingdom should be experienced. Jesus healed everyone who came to him. Miraculous healing is an integral part of demonstrating the kingdom realm. Jesus had compassion on people and wanted to heal them (Luke 5:12-13).

Miracles confirm the authenticity of Jesus and his kingdom realm. Jesus said miracles were a reason to believe he was who he said he was, the king of the kingdom (John 10:37-38). Jesus enabled the early disciples to perform miracles, "Paul and Barnabas spent considerable time there, speaking boldly for the Lord, who confirmed the message of his grace by enabling them to perform signs and wonders." (Acts 14:3).

If we want people to believe in Jesus, we will need to demonstrate the power of the kingdom realm, which includes signs, wonders, and miraculous healing. Supernatural miracles are possible because the same Spirit that raised Jesus from the dead is living in us (Romans 8:11). When Jesus performed miracles, it revealed his glory and led to people believing in him (John 2:23).

We regularly see miraculous healing when we pray for people. We also know of numerous other healing testimonies from other Christians across many denominations. We have lots of amazing stories from the many years we have been doing supernatural evangelism. Many who get healed will become Christians because they encountered the kingdom realm and king Jesus who healed them.

We live in a day where medical advances are rapid and there are medical solutions today that were not available to previous generations. But there are many diseases that still do not have a medical cure. Also, many people across the world do not have access or money to pay for what we in the UK can freely obtain from our National Health Service. Many people need a supernatural miracle to be healed.

We celebrate good healthcare and medical advances and the benefit that this brings humanity. We do not see it in competition with or a substitute for miraculous healing. Both are important to bring health and healing into people's lives. Miraculous healings will often cause people to believe in Jesus. We have both experienced Jesus' miraculous healing in our lives. It just makes us love him more and want to make him known.

"Yes, I do, why do you ask?"

Fiona was busy at work minding her own business. All a sudden she felt a sharp pain in her ear. Fiona knew her ear was ok, so she wondered whether a nearby tradesman repairing a window had a problem with his ear. Fiona went over to the tradesman and asked, "Do you have a problem with your ear?"

He said, "Yes I do, why do you ask?" Fiona explained that God had spoken to her because he cared for him and wanted to heal him. She then offered to pray for him. Somewhat surprised, the tradesman said he was suffering with Ménière's disease and was happy to be prayed for. Fiona then prayed that his ear would be healed, after which she went back to work.

Supernatural identity

A kingdom realm gospel includes God's love for us, that he wants us, desires to know us, and for us to know him. Only then can we feel truly complete, knowing our identity, purpose, and significance. Knowing that God wants to adopt us is a key part of the kingdom gospel (Galatians 4:4-5). Knowing we belong, are loved and are important are key needs only met in God.

Jesus often spoke to people about their identity. He told Nathanael that there was no deceit in his character. In response Nathanael asked how Jesus knew him. Jesus replied by saying he had seen him earlier under a fig tree. This was significant to Nathanael as he then recognised Jesus as the Son of God (John 1:47-49).

When Peter received revelation that Jesus was the Son of God, Jesus described Peter as a rock on which he will build the church. The Greek word for Peter[52] means rock. Using the meaning of his name, Jesus described how he saw Peter and the strength he had (Matthew 16:16-18).

Jesus knows us because we are his idea. He knows what we are like, our past, present and our future. He knows the plans he has created for us and the people we will become. He knows what is important to us and how we feel. Jesus may want to share these things with people as part of their journey to become a Christian.

"When you want your children to succeed you are being like God."

Mark was recently praying for an unbeliever who was part of an addict recovery programme. The unbeliever was painfully aware of his mistakes, failings, and regrets and how much his addiction had negatively impacted the people in his life. Considering this, the unbeliever wanted to know what God thought of him.

As Mark prayed, he discerned his low self-esteem and asked Holy Spirit how he should approach this. Holy Spirit said, "Affirm him that he wants his children to succeed". Mark first asked if he had children, which he did, and then said, "When you want your children to succeed you are being like God, who also wants his

---

[52] Petros, Strongs G4074, Peter means 'a rock or a stone.'

children to succeed."

The unbeliever had not thought this before and was somewhat caught out about God's positive view about him, considering his sense of failure for struggling with addiction. Mark was able to share more of God's heart for him and pray for an encounter with the Father's love.

For some people, knowing what God thinks of them will be a starting point for them in seeking to know more about the king and his kingdom realm.

Supernatural conviction

When we evangelise, it is unhelpful to think we can argue someone into becoming a Christian. Rather we should demonstrate the power of the gospel so that people's faith might not rest on human wisdom, but on God's power (1 Corinthians 2:5). Apologetics[53] has an important place in defending and explaining the gospel, but such arguments cannot be what people solely rest their faith on.

In the process of following Jesus and becoming a Christian, people's faith needs to rest on the supernatural power of God. For this to occur they need to see or experience the power of God. Having faith in Jesus is an essential part of the process in becoming a Christian. Through experiencing the kingdom realm, conviction[54] comes.

---

[53] en.wikipedia.org/wiki/Apologetics, the systematic defence of a religious position
[54] There are different ways to understand 1 Corinthians 2:1-5 and 1 Thessalonians 1:4-5, as to whether the Holy Spirit's power is referring to signs and wonders or conversion or both. Our intent here is to highlight the importance of both miracles and conviction within the salvation process. We do not include in this book a debate or comparison of the different theological viewpoints.

When Peter preached at Pentecost, people "were cut to the heart" (Acts 2:37) and ready to repent. Paul describes that when he brought the gospel to Thessalonica, it was not "simply with words but also with power, with the Holy Spirit and deep conviction." (1 Thessalonians 1:5).

Paul describes how prophecy in a church meeting can impact an unbeliever. It can result in them being convicted of sin and "the secrets of their hearts are laid bare" (1 Corinthians 14:25). What if 'the heart'[55] does not only relate to conviction of sin but also to people's identity, pain, needs, hopes, and dreams?

When people find out, through Christians bringing prophetic revelation, that God knows about their deepest desires it can bring about significant conviction that God is real.

"I am travelling at the moment to help me process the recent death of my father."

Mark was travelling in northern Europe as part of a team that was running a conference for several churches in the local area. The conference had finished, and the team were enjoying a tourist boat trip before they came home. Halfway through the trip, God drew Mark's attention to a man on the boat trip, telling him that the man had recently suffered a loss.

During the rest of the boat trip, Mark prayed about what God had said to be sure he understood it correctly. At the end of the trip, as they got off the boat, Mark asked the man if he had recently suffered a loss. The man replied, "I am travelling at the moment to help me process the recent death of my father."

---

[55] kardia, Strongs G2588, the soul or mind, as it is the fountain and seat of the thoughts, passions, desires, appetites, affections, purposes, endeavours, character, stirred in a bad way or good.

Mark shared with the man what God said and that God cared about him and knew how he was feeling. Mark prayed for the man to know God's comfort as he processed the death of his father. The man started to gently cry but was surprised and thankful, he also had a greater awareness of the reality of God.

Supernatural evangelistic moments

In recent history, as the number of Christians baptised in the Holy Spirit worldwide has grown, the number of people being born again has multiplied exponentially. In 1900[56] there were fewer than one million Pentecostal and Charismatic Christians. In 2011[57] there were an estimated 584 million Pentecostal and Charismatic Christians worldwide. Today[58] there are approximately 644 million Pentecostal and Charismatic Christians, which is expected to reach over 1 billion by 2050.

Between 1900 and today, the world population has grown nearly five times. During the same period, the number of Pentecostal and Charismatic Christians has grown over six hundred times! When the Holy Spirit was poured out at Pentecost, it ushered in a period of history which we are still in, where anyone who calls on the name of the Lord will be saved (Acts 2:21). Statistically, the more Christians that are baptised in the Spirit, the greater the number of people that are saved.

When Jesus preached and demonstrated the kingdom, he said to unbelievers the kingdom was near to them (Mark 1:15). By

[56] factsandtrends.net/2015/03/11/7-encouraging-trends-in-global-christianity/

[57] www.pewforum.org/2011/12/19/global-christianity-exec/

[58] www.catholicnewsagency.com/news/christians-by-number-what-projections-are-saying-about-the-future-of-religion-40092

preaching and supernaturally demonstrating the kingdom we show people they are within reach of God (Luke 10:9). Jesus' harvest of lost people is growing exponentially as more Christians are baptised in the Spirit and supernaturally demonstrate the good news of the kingdom.

Holy Spirit wants to invite us into supernatural evangelistic moments, whether it is through miracles, prophecy, healing, or love. Holy Spirit's activity in your life includes the power to bring in the harvest. Holy Spirit is working in people all around you, people you know and strangers you may come across.

God wants to open your eyes to see the evangelistic harvest all around you. He wants to give you evangelistic moments, so you can know the joy of sharing your faith and seeing supernatural miracles. We can learn to always be listening for Holy Spirit initiated evangelistic moments.

As we encounter God's supernatural presence, we can then lead unbelievers into supernatural encounters with his love and power. Partnering with God in his dream to reconcile the world to himself is to release the supernatural power of the kingdom realm into unbelievers' lives, so they can discover Jesus.

One of the reasons some Christians may find evangelism difficult is that they are taught evangelistic methods and tools that do not rely on Holy Spirit. To truly reveal the king and his kingdom realm requires supernatural evangelism. If we want to fully represent Jesus to unbelievers, it is best done by accessing the supernatural resources of heaven.

"She is an amazing individual."

When Fiona was working at a care home, there was a particularly difficult member of staff that she worked with called Shelley. All the other members of the team really struggled to get on with her. Shelley was very critical and pedantic, whenever another member of the team made the slightest error in their work she would go straight to the manager and tell them.

Lots of staff were fed up with Shelley and were gossiping, complaining, and moaning about her. The working environment got quite difficult; she made the working atmosphere somewhat tense when she was on shift. Whilst Fiona was on shift, she began to pray about it and asked God how he saw Shelley. God said, "She is an amazing individual, but because she carries so much emotional pain and hurt, and she has had so many things happen to her in her life, so few people will see that side of her."

When Fiona heard this, it changed her heart and perspective towards Shelley. Fiona continued to pray during her shift for Shelley. By the end of the shift, Fiona felt quite compelled to tell Shelley what God had shared with her. During a quiet moment, Fiona asked Shelley if she could chat with her alone. Fiona then shared with Shelley everything that God has said to her. On hearing this Shelley stood up, pushed her chair out, stomped out of the room and slammed the door behind her! Fiona thought to herself, "That didn't go well!"

Some weeks later, an agency worker Tina who was a Christian, was on shift with Fiona. Tina said to Fiona, "I heard about what happened with Shelley. There was lots of conversation about you in the staffroom." Fiona replied, "Oh dear, was there? What happened?" Tina said that Shelley had shared with the rest of the team exactly what Fiona had said to her. Tina asked Shelley, "How interesting, how did you feel when Fiona told you those things that she felt God had spoken to her about?"

Shelley's reply completely amazed Fiona. She said, "I was so surprised and so overwhelmed by what Fiona said, I thought I was going to burst into tears, but as I never cry in front of anybody, I thought I would get up and get out of the room as quickly as I could."

This was a huge lesson for Fiona to "walk by faith, not by sight" (2 Corinthians 5:7, NKJV), and to be able to impact someone for the gospel without having any positive feedback on the spot. At the time Fiona thought the conversation with Shelley was a disaster. She also learnt not to worry about taking an evangelistic risk, even though she may be the talk of the staffroom for a while!

Activation

Reflect on this verse:

> *And everyone who calls on the name of the Lord will be saved.*
>
> Acts 2:21

Ask God:

- Do I fully understand what it means to be baptised in the Holy Spirit?
- How can I recognise evangelistic moments around me?
- How can I supernaturally share your love and compassion for unbelievers around me?

Pray:

> *Father, thank you that you want to empower me to bring in the harvest. I pray you would baptise me in the Spirit. Please fill me with your love and power. Enable me to do signs and wonders and give me courage to pray for those who need a miracle.*

To do:

- Write down what God said to you and meditate on it.
- This week, why don't you offer to pray for a family member, friend or work colleague who needs miraculous healing? Pray for a need that you see or that Holy Spirit may tell you about.

Further reading:

- John 4:5-26
- John 10:37-38
- 1 Peter 1:10-12

CHOOSING JESUS

If I am to wholly follow the Lord Jesus Christ, I must
forsake everything that is contrary to Him.
(W. Tozer, Pastor and Author)

"It's me you want, I am thinking of becoming a Christian."

When our children were young, we were driving home from a weekend away with friends. During the journey one of our children was sick and an unpleasant odour filled the car! Fortunately, the next service station was only a few miles away, so we stopped to change our child's clothes and get some cleaning materials for the car.

As Mark approached the checkout, Holy Spirit said to him that the shop assistant was close to salvation. As he paid for the goods, Mark asked the sales assistant "Are you thinking of becoming a Christian?" "No," she replied, somewhat surprised at the question.

Then the shop assistant at the adjacent till said, "It's me you want, I am thinking of becoming a Christian." The shop assistant went on to explain that one of her friends had been asking her to church for weeks, but she had yet to accept. Mark replied, "I think you should go to church with your friend the next time they ask you."

Mark shared with the shop assistant about how God was drawing her to himself and how he wanted to have a relationship with her.

He encouraged the shop assistant to seek God and try talking to him. On the way back to the car Mark was full of joy and clearing up the sick suddenly didn't seem such a big deal!

Making Disciples

More people are coming to Christ every day than at any other time in history. The Apostle Paul says, "I tell you, now is the time of God's favour, now is the day of salvation." (2 Corinthians 6:2). As unbelievers encounter Jesus and his kingdom realm, many will want to follow him. As they do, Jesus wants them to become his disciples (Matthew 28:19).

Follow the leader[59] is a traditional children's game where children line up behind a leader and the mimic their actions. Any children who do not follow what the leader does are out of the game. The game is popular in many cultures and referenced in films, music, and literature.

In the Galilean Rabbinic school system, children were educated with the goal that the best students would become a rabbi. Students who did not make the cut at either age ten or fifteen would return home and learn their father's trade. Those who continued would further study until they were thirty, at which point they would be recognised as a rabbi. It is highly likely Jesus went through the Rabbinic school system.

When you became a rabbi, you would look for students who you thought would have the ability to emulate you and imitate you. When Jesus asked people to follow him, he was doing it within a

---

[59] en.wikipedia.org/wiki/Follow_the_leader_(game)

culture that understood that nuanced call. In their culture, 'follow me' was a call to discipleship, where a student would study the life, beliefs, values, and behaviour of a rabbi, so they could mimic them and change their life to become like them.

Ann Spangler and Lois Tverberd describe it like this: "The mission of a rabbi was to become a living example of what it means to apply God's Word to one's life. A disciple apprenticed himself to a rabbi because the rabbi had saturated his life with Scripture and had become a true follower of God. The disciple sought to study the text, not only of Scripture, but of the rabbi's life, for it was there that he would learn how to live out the Torah. Even more than acquiring his master's knowledge, he wanted to acquire his master's character, his internal grasp of God's law."[60]

When Jesus asked Peter, Andrew, James, and John to follow him, they were working as fishermen, implying that they had at some point dropped out of school (Matthew 4:18-22). Jesus was calling them as a rabbi[61], which is why they left their trade and father and followed him. In this Jewish context, these 'dropouts' were invited by a rabbi to follow him, which was a great honour. When they received such an invitation it was culturally normal to leave their work and family to do so.

This Rabbinic discipleship call by Jesus should not be mistaken with what we might describe today as a 'call to salvation'. When the first disciples chose to follow rabbi Jesus, they did it to study his life so they could, in time, become like him. They did not become

---

[60]Ann Spangler and Lois Tverberd, Sitting at the Feet of rabbi Jesus: How the Jewishness of Jesus Can Transform Your Faith (2009).

[61] Peter, Judas and Nathanael call Jesus rabbi in Mark 9:5, Matthew 26:25 and John 1:38, see rhabbi, Strongs G4461

Christians at this moment. It was some years later that the first disciples came to know through revelation that Jesus was the Messiah. Even so, they understood Jesus' invitation was a call to discipleship.

As people encounter him and his kingdom, Jesus is looking for people to realise its true value and give all that they have for it (Matthew 13:44-46). This was the prime motivation Jesus gave for repentance. Understanding this affects how we will help people choose Jesus, follow him, and become his disciples.

Phrases such as 'asking Jesus into my life' don't really capture what it means to enter the kingdom realm and become a disciple. Jesus asks us into his transformational resurrection life (Romans 6:4-5) so we can know him and live a supernatural lifestyle, demonstrating his kingdom realm any time, any place, anywhere. The Greek word for disciple 'mathētēs'[62] significantly appears over 250 times within the New Testament.

Our focus should not be getting converts over the line, but making disciples who will give their all for Jesus and his kingdom realm. God's dream to reconcile the world to himself includes the church becoming his bride. At the end of time Jesus marries his bride, who has made herself ready for him (Revelation 19:7-9). Jesus also prepares his bride to be radiant, blameless and without blemish (Ephesians 5:25-27).

This is a powerful description of the church, which is the context of discipleship. God reconciles people to himself so that he can put new disciples in thriving healthy churches. Within churches,

---

[62] blueletterbible.org/lang/lexicon/lexicon.cfm?Strongs=G3101

disciples can live in unity and maturity, representing Christ fully (Ephesians 4:11-16). Being a disciple involves life-long learning and growth, alongside other disciples on the same journey. Only together can we truly represent Christ fully to the world.

Rushing people to become Christians can be counterproductive. A premature baby is not usually healthy and will need intensive care. During evangelism we are presenting a choice for Jesus and his kingdom, a choice to become his disciple. We should not encourage people to make this decision lightly. If we do, we won't set people up for success in their Christian life, and they may struggle or give up.

Ann Spangler and Lois Tverberd state: "So often we focus on Jesus's mission on the cross to save us from our sins. As marvellous as that is, it's critical for us to grasp the importance of his mission on earth as a rabbi. His goal was to raise up disciples who would become like him. As followers of Jesus, we are still called to live out the adventure of discipleship, becoming like Jesus through the power of his Spirit at work within us."[63]

What about hell?

As we introduce unbelievers to Jesus and his kingdom ream, it is important to consider how hell fits within a message about the good news of the kingdom. It may surprise you, but Jesus did not speak frequently about the subject of hell with unbelievers. Most of Jesus' discussions and parables about hell were with his disciples. The same was true of the apostles; most of their references to hell and judgement are in letters to churches and in the book of Revelation.

---

[63] Ann Spangler and Lois Tverberd, Sitting at the Feet of rabbi Jesus: How the Jewishness of Jesus Can Transform Your Faith (2009).

For example, in the parable of the Sheep and the Goats (Matthew 25:31-46), Jesus is speaking privately to his disciples at the Mount of Olives. Also, in the parable of the Rich Man and Lazarus (Luke 16:19-31), Jesus is teaching his disciples.

The theological understanding of hell is progressive throughout the Bible. The Old Testament uses a concept called Shoel[64], whereas the New Testament uses concepts such as Hades[65] and Gehenna[66]. Each of these concepts develop into a fuller understanding of what hell is, culminating in Jesus' teaching and the book of Revelation.

The Bible defines 'Hades' as the place where unbelievers go when they die whilst they wait for judgement (Luke 16:23). After judgement day, Hades (the realm of the dead) gets thrown in the lake of fire (Revelation 20:11-14). The Bible uses terms 'eternal punishment', 'eternal fire' and 'lake of fire' to describe the second death (Revelation 2:11, 20:6 and 21:8).

The 'lake of fire', which is eternal punishment, is commonly referred to and understood as hell. Eternal fire is created for the devil and his angels (Matthew 25:41), and those who refuse to love the truth of the gospel (2 Thessalonians 2:9-10).

Where hell, judgement or eternal punishment is mentioned with unbelievers they are almost exclusively mentioned when speaking to a crowd. Biblical examples are The Sermon on the Mount, Jesus' judgement of the Pharisees' religiosity and hypocrisy[67] and Jesus' judgement of unrepentant cities[68].

---

[64] Shoel is the grave, the world of the dead, see shĕowl, Strongs H7585

[65] Hades is the place of departed souls, see hadēs, Strongs G86

[66] Gehenna is a valley in Jerusalem that is used figuratively for hell, see geenna, Strongs G1067

[67] Pharisees religiosity and hypocrisy examples include Matthew 12:1-45, Matthew 23:1-38, Luke 11:37-54, and John 8:12-59.

[68] Judgement of unrepentant cities examples include Matthew 11:20-24, and Luke 11:29-32.

In these scenarios Jesus is addressing three groups of people: the self-righteous (Luke 16:19-31), those looking to reduce the significance of their sin (Luke 13:1-5) and those who do the desires of the devil (John 8:44-45). The apostles also follow the same approach, only speaking about hell and judgement to crowds. Biblical examples include Peter speaking with Cornelius' family and servants (Acts 10:42) and Paul speaking in Athens at the Areopagus (Acts 17:31).

There is only one evangelistic conversation with an individual in the Gospels and Book of Acts that includes any reference to hell or judgement. This conversation is between Jesus and Nicodemus, who later followed Jesus and became a Christian (John 3:14-21).

It is important to note that the conversation between Jesus and Nicodemus starts with Nicodemus making the statement: "Rabbi, we know that you are a teacher who has come from God. For no one could perform the signs you are doing if God were not with him." (John 3:2).

This statement implies that Nicodemus had previously seen and heard the reality of Jesus' kingdom realm. This is also true of the other examples above where Jesus and the apostles preached to crowds or had conversations with groups of people within the crowds. They had all previously heard, seen, or experienced miracles by Jesus or the apostles.

During this conversation, Jesus answered Nicodemus' questions and explained who he is and why he came. Even though Jesus mentioned judgement and perishing, he said it in the context of why he had been sent to save the world, not to condemn it (John 3:17).

Any mention of hell and judgement with unbelievers in the Bible is usually preceded with speaking about and demonstrating the kingdom realm. Kingdom realm analogies (parables) about who Jesus is, his love for people, his desire to forgive and rescue people, and supernatural miracles usually came before any mention of hell and judgement. It is also worth noting that hell and judgement are not mentioned in most of the messages to crowds or conversations with individuals.

Though Jesus rarely mentioned hell and judgement with individuals, he did sometimes speak to an individual about their sin, if it was going to stop them repenting and following him[69]. This is an important distinction. Jesus does not, for an individual, use hell or judgement as a motivation for repentance, but Jesus does challenge specific sin in some people's lives where it is a stumbling block to them entering the kingdom realm.

Based on these passages it is difficult to create a Biblical case for using hell as the *primary* motivator, or reason for repentance in a gospel message to unbelievers. Though it can have a place when speaking with crowds and the self-righteous, our evangelistic focus for most people should be on revealing and demonstrating Jesus and his kingdom realm.

Using evangelism methods that focus on conversion rather than on discipleship may have a greater focus on hell than Jesus did. For example, asking eternity questions to unbelievers as a starting point of an evangelistic conversation. An example question would be, "If you were to die tonight, do you know where you would go?" Whilst they can generate good conversations, they may end up focusing on

---

[69] Examples of individual sin include John 5:1-15, John 8:1-11, Mark 10:17-22, and Luke 9:57-62.

sin and hell. Jesus' starting point was to introduce the reality and nearness of the kingdom realm.

Such methods can also lead people to become a Christian out of fear, before they find out who Jesus is and why he is worth following. Using fear as a motivation for repentance has the danger of people becoming Christians out of self-preservation rather than a true change of heart to follow Jesus. The sad result can be they later fall away, because their foundation for becoming a Christian was the fear of going to hell rather than God's love, acceptance, and forgiveness.

Richard Halverson[70] said, "Evangelism is not salesmanship. It is not urging people, pressing them, coercing them, overwhelming them, or subduing them. Evangelism is telling a message. Evangelism is reporting good news."

Repentance and believing

Choosing Jesus requires repentance. Jesus' motivation for people to repent was because the kingdom realm was within reach (Matthew 4:17); it was not the fear of hell. Jesus preached, "The kingdom of God has come near. Repent and believe the good news". (Mark 1:15).

John the Baptist also preached repentance because the kingdom of heaven had come near (Matthew 3:1-2). Jesus also asks us to go into all the nations and preach repentance for the forgiveness of sins (Luke 24:47). Repentance is a central part of the kingdom gospel.

---

[70] en.wikipedia.org/wiki/Richard_C._Halverson

As Jesus healed people, drove out demons, gave hope, taught, and discipled, people experienced his kingdom realm. As people experience the reality of the kingdom realm, Jesus expected and longed for people to repent. When they didn't repent, he denounced towns in which some of his miracles had been performed (Matthew 11:20-21) and left them no excuse for their sin (John 15:22-24).

The meaning of repent in the English dictionary[71] is to feel or express regret or remorse for sin, but the Bible defines repentance as a change of mind, to think differently, to comprehend, to reconsider[72]. Repentance involves not just being sorry for our sin but leaving our life of sin behind (John 8:11). Repentance is a fundamental inward transformation in our thinking, beliefs, and values, which in turn affects our behaviour.

This may involve openly confessing our sin and breaking from our past by ridding our lives of unhelpful influences[73]. It could also involve putting things right, such as returning money that has been stolen, stopping sexual relationships outside of marriage, leaving a damaging addictive lifestyle, repairing relationships we have damaged, forgiving others, and seeking forgiveness from those we have wronged.

Repentance of sin leads to forgiveness, which is good news because we are no longer condemned. We are then redeemed from all wickedness, we are purified, and become eager to do what is good (Titus 2:14). We enter the kingdom of God through being born again. We receive eternal life, which means to know God (John 17:3), now and for eternity (John 14:2-4).

---

[71] www.dictionary.com/browse/repentance
[72] metanoia, Strongs G3341, metanoeō, Strongs G3340 and noeō, Strongs G3539
[73] For example, burning sorcery books in Acts 19:18-19.

Repentance also involves believing in who Jesus is, what he has done, and what he says is true. Biblical faith and belief are not blind faith, they are about being persuaded[74], having conviction of truth, placing confidence in[75], trusting in[76], and relying on Jesus, who he is, what he has achieved and what he says is true[77].

We repent *from* sin and turn *to* Jesus, because sin stops us believing in Jesus (John 16:9). Jesus rejoices when Peter tells him he is the Son of the living God. Jesus then points out that Peter only knows this because Father God revealed this to him (Matthew 16:16-17). The kingdom realm's focus is to connect people to Jesus, so they can see who he really is, believe in him and know the truth.

When we repent, we receive his righteousness through faith (Romans 3:22), knowing that our own righteousness is not enough. We also repent about believing the lies of the devil (John 8:44), knowing that God is good, and that Jesus has come to bring us life to the full (John 10:10).

Many unbelievers think that God is angry, distant, uncaring and the author of sickness. In other words, they don't believe God is good. They also may have low self-image because they have believed lies about themselves. Repentance towards Jesus, who is the truth (John 14:6) will bring freedom into our lives (John 8:32-36).

Repenting and becoming a disciple may mean that we may face persecution as a Christian (2 Timothy 3:12). Discipleship can mean we may face hardship and loss for the sake of Christ (Mark 10:29-30). Repentance means making Jesus the most important thing in our life.

---

[74] pistis, Strongs G4102
[75] pisteuō, Strongs G4100
[76] pistikos, Strongs G4101
[77] pistos, Strongs G4103

Leading unbelievers in repentance is one of the greatest privileges of our lives. Helping them in biblical repentance will be the most effective start to their new life in Christ. Repentance focuses on becoming a disciple of Jesus, not simply conversion. Introducing people to Jesus and his kingdom is the most effective way for people to discover the pearl of great price, which they will give all they have for (Matthew 13:44-46).

Repentance needs to lead to a clear commitment and confession of faith. When we lead people in repentance, we take time to pray with them individually. Throughout the whole process we are listening to Holy Spirit for his direction. We start by validating that they want to become a Christian, have counted the cost and understand what repentance means.

Jesus compares this decision to count the cost as someone building a tower needing to assess that they have enough money to complete it and a king who evaluates whether he has enough soldiers to win a war (Luke 14:25-35). Despite the large crowds following him, Jesus challenged them to see if they wanted to be his disciples. Repentance is about choosing a life of discipleship.

We then lead them in a prayer of repentance where we ask them to pray out loud, "If you declare with your mouth, 'Jesus is Lord,' and believe in your heart that God raised him from the dead, you will be saved" (Romans 10:9). We ask if there is any specific sin that God has brought to their mind that they need to repent of. If there is, we get them to confess the sin out loud and agree to put it right (e.g. return money stolen) or get rid of unhelpful influences (e.g. pornographic material).

After the prayer we will ask them if they need to forgive anyone.

If there is, we will ask them to forgive them. Forgiveness is part of repentance and is not something that should be skipped over. We then encourage them to speak to anyone they have offended and look for opportunity to repair any broken relationships.

We then ask them if they have been involved in any demonic activity. If there has been, we ask them to repent of it out loud. We will pray and break off any demonic influence. We encourage them that going forward Jesus is their only spiritual source and suggest getting rid of any occult books or artefacts that they have.

We pray with them to be baptised in the Holy Spirit. Because they have experienced Jesus and his kingdom on their journey to this point, they have an expectation that something real and amazing will happen. During this time, we ask them what they feel and are experiencing, so we can discern what God is doing. It is common for people to experience deep or new emotions, feel God's presence in their body, speak in tongues, hear God speak to them, and prophesy.

To finish, we will encourage them to tell someone before the day's end that they have become a Christian. Sharing such good news helps cement the decision they have made. We will also encourage them to be baptised in water (Acts 2:38), inviting friends, family, neighbours, and work colleagues to the celebratory occasion, which symbolises death of the old self and the beginning of a new life in Christ (Romans 6:4).

Joining God's Family

When we become Christians, we become children of God and join his family. Jesus taught us to pray to 'Our Father in heaven' (Matthew 6:9). He asked us to pray to the heavenly Father we all have in common. A family is God's design where children are nurtured from infants to adults, a place where they can confidently learn, and a safe place to make mistakes. The church is God's family, where the same holds true for new Christians. Discipleship occurs within the context of family.

We have found that integrating new Christians into a local church is key to their faith getting rooted and established. The first five years of a child's life are important for several reasons[78]. A child's brain develops rapidly during their first five years of life; it is a time of rapid cognitive, linguistic, social, emotional, and motor development. These years define and provide a foundation for their self-confidence, self-esteem, and their identity.

If a new Christian is welcomed into a healthy church, that cares and disciples them they are more likely to flourish in their Christian life. Sharing a common journey with others being discipled (like siblings) provides a common sense of purpose and identity, meaning they feel emotionally that they belong to a spiritual home.

A healthy church will intentionally disciple new believers and integrate them relationally into their church. Like a child's first five years of development, establishing a new Christian's identity in Christ within the early years is equally important. Dedicating time to discipling new believers will lead to more mature believers (2 Peter 1:3-10) that will actively take part in God's dream to reconcile the world to himself.

Jesus came to set us free, so any discipleship should include freedom in every area of our life. The Hebrew word for saved[79] means to

---

[78] www.factsforlifeglobal.org/03/1.html

[79] sōzō, Strongs G4982, example uses of the word saved include Matthew 1:21, Matthew 9:22, Mark 5:28 and Mark 5:34.

save, deliver, and heal. Salvation is more than just saving us from our sins. God brings freedom in how we think and how we feel, in our body, and in our spirit.

Freedom is also about being ourselves as God designed us, living without burdens or limitations. Freedom also means giving young Christians time to grow and not putting on them unrealistic expectations to always get it right. No child becomes an adult overnight!

Discipleship of new believers requires opportunity to put their faith into practice and not just include good teaching. We have watched with delight as new Christians happily engage in supernatural evangelism, without some of the 'baggage' that older Christians can have. It is a joy to share their excitement of seeing their first miracle when they prayed for someone's healing, hearing God's voice directing them during an evangelistic moment, and leading their first person to Christ.

"There is a way to God? Why has no-one ever told me?"

Mark was at a national spiritualist event with other Christians, looking for opportunities to introduce spiritually hungry people to Jesus and his kingdom realm. During a break, Mark was looking around at the various stalls. At one stall he got into conversation with the stallholder, who offered him a free session as a fellow stallholder to help him discover his destiny.

Mark replied that he already knew his identity and his destiny. The spiritualist was intrigued by his confidence. Mark declined the offer of a free session but offered them a free session in return. The spiritualist didn't know that the team Mark was part of didn't charge any money for sessions. Mark was using the offer to create ıity for the gospel.

Later the spiritualist came to have the free session. At the session people were asked to pick a card on a table that they were drawn to. Each card had a picture on top and a Bible verse on the underside, which was the basis to start a conversation with the visitor to the stall.

The spiritualist chose a card from a selection on the table that had the verse, "I am the way and the truth and the life. No one comes to the Father except through me." (John 14:6). Her response was astonishing, "There is a way to God? Why has no-one ever told me?" Mark explained the way to God was through Jesus, his life, death, and resurrection. He was able to pray for her to encounter God and encourage her to read more about Jesus in the Bible.

There are many people in our society that are hungry for truth, genuine spiritual experience, identity, destiny, and freedom. God wants to send us to such people, to introduce them to Jesus and his kingdom realm. Jesus' pursuit of people is bigger than our evangelistic efforts. Holy Spirit is already working in people's lives through conviction (John 16:8), creation (Romans 1:20), and visions (Acts 10:3). We get to join in with what he is already doing.

Activation

Reflect on this verse:

> *Very truly I tell you, no one can enter the kingdom of God unless they are born of water and the Spirit. Flesh gives birth to flesh, but the Spirit gives birth to spirit. You should not be surprised at my saying, "You must be born again."*
>
> John 3:5-7

Ask God:

- Do I fully understand what it means to choose Jesus?
- Is my evangelism focused on disciples or converts?
- How can I share your kingdom realm with unbelieving family, friends, work colleagues and others around me?

Pray:

> *Father, thank you for the gift of repentance, the forgiveness of sin and the ability to know you. Help me to lead many in repentance and the call to discipleship. I pray for my church to thrive, be healthy and mature as it plays its part in becoming your bride.*

To do:

- Write down what God said to you and meditate on it.
- This week, why don't you offer to pray for a person you meet who needs miraculous healing? Pray for a need that you see or that Holy Spirit may tell you about.

Further reading:

- Matthew 11:20-21
- Matthew 13:44-46
- Revelation 19:7-9

GOD'S DREAM

THE EVANGELIST

Given that my title at Google is Chief Internet Evangelist, I feel like there is this great challenge before me because we have three billion users, and there are seven billion people in the world.
(Vint Cerf, Internet Pioneer)

"Him Upstairs."

Fiona was out on a Friday evening waiting to meet up with a friend. Whilst she waited, she met a man who also seemed to be waiting for someone. They started talking and after a few minutes, Fiona asked him about his interesting collection of piercings he had in his left ear. He said each one had a story behind it.

The safety pin in his ear was a reminder of his misspent youth and his 'punk rocker' years. Fiona asked him about the leather cross earring he had. He remarked that it was a nod to 'him upstairs'. Fiona asked him to explain what he meant by that.

Ten years before a car had hit him whilst he crossed a road late at night. The car drove away leaving him alone in the middle of the road. Somebody found him and rang an ambulance. He was taken to hospital and it was a 'miracle' he survived. All his left side was 'mashed' and he had metal pins put in his leg and was unable to lift his left arm higher than his shoulder.

Fiona shared with him healing stories of people she knew who had metal disappear from their bodies after prayer, some of which had been verified by x-rays. The man was intrigued, amazed, and interested by these miracle stories. Fiona then offered to pray for him for healing and he accepted.

Fiona prayed for the metal in his body to disappear and that his pain would go. She then offered to pray for his arm to have full movement restored. He responded by saying there was no point because he could not lift it above his shoulder. Fiona then said, "Him upstairs, he really loves you, and the fact that you are still here tells you that he cares about you."

The man agreed to accept Fiona's prayer for his arm. She put her hand on his shoulder and prayed for a few seconds that his shoulder would be healed in Jesus' name and he would get full mobility. After praying, Fiona asked him to try it out.

With a very surprised expression he said, "No way, what the **** just happened there!" as he lifted his arm straight up above his head for the first time in ten years! Fiona then explained that 'Him upstairs' had saved his life that night many years ago and that Jesus is still in the business of doing miracles.

Are all Christians evangelists?

Our daughter was Skyping a university friend to plan an event. They were both part of their university Christian Union Executive Committee. Mark interrupted her, as he needed to briefly speak to her about something important. After their short conversation he took the opportunity to say hello to her friend. As he left the conversation, Holy Spirit spoke to him about her friend. Mark turned around and rejoined the Skype conversation.

Mark asked our daughter's friend, "Do you have a dream to work for a church as an evangelist?" He replied, "Yes, but I am not sure what an evangelist is." Mark had a brief conversation about who the evangelist is, after which our daughter's friend said, "Aren't all Christians evangelists?" Though not all Christians are evangelists, our daughter's friend was thinking like an evangelist; all Christians can be evangelistic. How we are wired and how we think can help us understand which gifts God has given us.

Mark was once speaking with a visitor at our church who was interested in evangelism training. Mark asked, "Do you think of yourself as an evangelist?" The person replied, "I am not sure, but aren't all Christians evangelists?" The person thought the same as our daughter's friend. They both did not realise that they themselves were evangelists. Mark then asked, "Do you want to equip Christians to do evangelism?" They replied, "Yes, how did you know that?" Mark replied, "This is how evangelists think because it is part of what they do."

Often when people are asked to name evangelists, they typically mention famous people who have preached to millions of people. When we do name evangelists, it will indicate how we define them and what attributes in their lives are relevant to being one. Church denominations can also have specific roles and expectations for an evangelist.

The Apostle Paul writes, "Christ himself gave the apostles, the prophets, the evangelists, the pastors and teachers, to equip his people for works of service, so that the body of Christ may be built up until we all reach unity in the faith and in the knowledge of the

Son of God and become mature, attaining to the whole measure of the fullness of Christ" (Ephesians 4:11-13).

God has given these gifts of people to the church to nurture, equip, bring unity, build up the church, and grow it to maturity. God's desire for the church has always been that it will grow and reach maturity, and be filled with the presence, power and riches of Christ. To achieve this, God has designed five important gifts that play a unique part in bringing maturity to the church[80].

A common idea of the evangelist is often 'the one who does evangelism', but that is not how the Bible defines the gift. Yes, doing evangelism is part of what they do, but the Bible defines these gifts, including the evangelist gift, by their ability to equip and nurture. It is important to define the evangelist as the Bible does, as otherwise we won't be able to recognise the gift in people and help them to embrace it.

Missional Foundations

The church is the house of God that is "built on the foundation of the apostles and prophets, with Christ Jesus himself as the chief cornerstone." (Ephesians 2:20). The church was founded on its identity as the Family of God (Matthew 12:49-50), the Bride of Christ (Ephesians 5:32) and the Temple of the Holy Spirit (1 Corinthians 3:16-17).

The church was also founded on its missional purpose to be the Light of the World (Matthew 5:14-16), knowing it has been sent by Jesus to seek and save the lost (John 20:21-22). Christians who

---

[80] To read more about the Ephesians 4 gifts, we recommend the book Culture of Honor (2013), by Danny Silk.

recognise their missional foundation will, whatever their circumstances and wherever they are, demonstrate the kingdom realm and preach the gospel (Acts 8:4).

The apostles and prophets help Christians understand their identity and missional purpose. In other words, they help people embrace the culture and priorities of the kingdom realm. One of the priorities of the kingdom realm is the Great Commission.

The word 'apostle'[81] means a delegate, messenger, one sent forth with orders and the term is borrowed from the Roman Empire. In Greek culture, an apostle was an emissary sent by the Emperor to represent and cultivate the culture of Rome within a newly conquered province or country.

Roman apostles would bring the culture of their native environment with the purpose to influence and transform the area into which they had been sent. They would do this to such an extent that if the ruler of the sending nation were to visit the newly conquered area, they would feel 'at home'. Christian apostles represent and cultivate the culture of heaven's kingdom realm within Christians, churches, and the world.

The two people in the Book of Acts that undertake the most evangelism are Peter and Paul. Neither of these two is described in the Bible as evangelists; they are both called apostles. The ministry of the apostles regularly touched unbelievers[82] and it included preaching the gospel in many places. The apostles took up the Great Commission; advancing the gospel was one of their priorities (Philippians 1:12).

---

[81] apostolos, Strongs G652
[82] Examples of the Apostles preaching to unbelievers include Acts 5:12-16 and Acts 8:25.

The apostles and the evangelists work together to advance the gospel. In Samaria, Philip the evangelist preached and demonstrated the kingdom realm. Those who believed were baptised. When the apostles in Jerusalem heard what had happened in Samaria, they sent Peter and John. When they arrived, they placed their hands on the new believers and they received the Holy Spirit (Acts 8:14-17).

Evangelists (and pastors and teachers) are designed to operate in churches that have grasped their missional identity and purpose. This is the context in which the evangelist motivates and equips people to partner with God to bring about God's dream to reconcile the world to himself. Within this context, evangelists can thrive and help build evangelistic culture and community.

Janice

From childhood I had been involved in traditional approaches to evangelism, such as leading a good life, going door-to-door in my neighbourhood and street preaching. I often explained the steps to salvation to friends and family, trying by persuasion or argument to get them to say a salvation prayer, or trying to soberly scare someone with the question, "If you died tonight, where do you think you would go?"

Whilst a university Christian Union Hall Rep, we saw forty-two people saved in the first term, following a previous term of persistently praying with a friend for the first-year students who would move into their hall of residence.

When I was a young solicitor, I broke my back and was due multiple operations with a prognosis that I would be in a wheelchair by the time I was 30 years old. God had other plans and I was miraculously and instantaneously healed when prayed for at a healing meeting. About ten of my relatives and friends became Christians as a direct result.

A few years later, I broke my shoulder whilst in a car crash. The prognosis by a top London Harley Street orthopaedic surgeon was that I would be permanently disabled. God miraculously healed my arm, as a result ten colleagues gave their lives to Jesus and everyone in my department (more than forty people) came to church with me.

After this, I went into over twenty years of a spiritual wilderness experience as far as evangelism was concerned. I got more and more caught up with work as a lawyer and found fewer and fewer opportunities to witness. In those years I shared my faith with a handful of close colleagues but without any obvious fruit.

The evangelistic drought ended abruptly when in the autumn of 2017 I started the first year in Eastgate School of Spiritual Life (ESSL). Within weeks I was challenged by new approaches to evangelism that embraced a lighter touch through all the weekly outreach activities.

Although in the first weeks I struggled with Treasure Hunting and the prophetic activities, I found that following an "Excuse me..." people did stop and were interested or intrigued, and opportunities immediately arose to pray with them on the streets.

Later that term, a visiting speaker said to me, "God is doing something really powerful in your life. I don't know what it is, but it's really powerful." He then asked me to hold his hands, at which point I felt a surge of power go through me. Over the next five days

I saw five people healed on the streets as I interrupted their days with kindness and offered to pray for them.

Through the subsequent revelatory teaching in the school on evangelism, miraculous healing, and hearing from God, I found that this spiritual fruit wasn't, as was the case at other points in my life, just a special event. I realised that I could be supernaturally natural every day, every week for the rest of my life.

The turning point for me was in Fiona's classes based on Romans 2:4, when I grasped, "It's the kindness of God that leads to repentance." Not the threat of hell or the condemnation of peoples' sins. I discovered that God is speaking to us all the time and when we tune in, we can hear what He is saying about and for the people around us. I realised others could encounter God through me.

Compared with my previous evangelistic 'good intentions' where I would seek to argue, persuade and pressurise people into becoming a Christian, I learnt that everybody I meet is on a journey and that, quite to the contrary, I didn't have to feel pressure to get the salvation message across. My witness may just be a step on their journey to salvation. Fiona asked me to think about how many steps it took before I came to Christ.

So instead I began simply to expect something good to happen to people because Christ is in me. In Jesus' day people got to know him as the Healer, the Prophet, the Provider before they necessarily followed Him.

I began to understand that if I went up to someone or stopped someone, I was not an inconvenience; I was punctuating their day with goodness, kindness, healing, etc. I slowly realised that the prophetic is a harvesting tool. What followed was a slow but steady build-up of courage as I began to hear from Holy Spirit through a picture or a word and then pushed through my natural British reserve with strangers.

I started to take a 'running leap' across what appeared to be a huge psychological chasm by saying "Excuse me…" to a stranger when I felt I had a picture or word to share with them, only to discover that once I had engaged with them, the chasm was in fact a tiny hop and Holy Spirit was immediately there with me, backing me up and engineering an encounter with someone in a profoundly supernaturally natural way, that only he can achieve.

Initially I found it hard, to cope with my heart pounding and my head screaming lies, such as, "Don't do it, you'll mess up, they'll think you're odd and be put off Christianity for good, it won't work," and so on. I found that peace and confidence steadily grew as I began to have actual testimonies of people being touched, healed, or saved. As I shared my stories with my fellow ESSL students, amazingly, evangelistic opportunities grew.

My testimony is that it's a lot easier than we think to be evangelistic when we rely on Holy Spirit, as then we don't have to perform, we don't bring ministry, it's already happening, we're just joining God in the process. It's not just proclaiming the gospel, it's demonstrating the kingdom. It's the 'show and tell' of the gospel and it's a far better way!

The evangelist's strengths

The evangelist Billy Graham[83] said, "One of the greatest priorities of

---

[83] en.wikipedia.org/wiki/Billy_Graham

the church today is to mobilize the laity to do the work of evangelism." The evangelist gift is made up of five areas of strength:

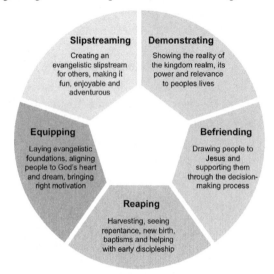

Evangelists will have all five strengths within them but may be relatively stronger in one or more of them. All the five strengths are important and contribute to the full picture of what the evangelist gift is. Building an evangelism team with strengths in all five areas will bring a greater kingdom impact and evangelistic maturity within churches.

Some definitions of the evangelist gift can be limited to one or two of these strengths. This can lead to people having a distorted view of the evangelist gift or questioning whether they are evangelists, because they have used a narrow definition of the gift.

For example, if a definition of an evangelist focuses on just doing evangelism, they may not fully utilise their gift by equipping Christians. God has designed the gift much more widely, so it's important to recognise all its strengths, to value them all and to help people mature in them.

These strengths apply regardless of role or title. An evangelist can equip many or few. They don't need to be in a leadership role to nurture and equip people. It's time to reimagine the creativity and passion carried by the evangelist gift to bring people to Christ and joyfully equip the church to live evangelistic lifestyles.

Having God's perspective on the evangelist gift is key to fulfilling his dream.

Demonstrating

This strength is about showing unbelievers the nearness and reality of the kingdom realm, its relevance to their lives and how it works. This may involve healing, miracles, prophecy, discussion, debate, apologetics, or love encounters with Jesus.

In Acts, nearly all new evangelistic groundbreaking starts with *God's initiation* through a vision, the voice of Holy Spirit, or an angel. We see this with the evangelist Philip, first in Samaria and then on the desert road between Jerusalem and Gaza.

In Samaria, Philip the evangelist preaches and demonstrates the kingdom realm. "When the crowds heard Philip and saw the signs he performed, they all paid close attention to what he said. For with shrieks, impure spirits came out of many, and many who were paralysed or lame were healed. So there was great joy in that city." (Acts 8:6-8).

In this passage, the evangelist proclaims the gospel of the kingdom, miraculously heals people, and casts out demons. Such was Philip's impact that many people were healed and there was great joy in the city. Philip also baptised those who believed: "when they believed Philip as he proclaimed the good news of the kingdom of God and the name of Jesus Christ, they were baptised, both men and women." (Acts 8:12).

Befriending

This strength provides support and companionship to people throughout their journey to faith. It encourages people to find out more about Jesus and spends time with them answering their questions, showing compassion, regularly praying for them, and putting God's kindness on display.

Evangelists are motivated by God's love and compassion for those who are not yet children of God. Jesus regularly had compassion and this is evident throughout the Gospels. Whether he was teaching people through parables or healing the sick, he showed compassion[84].

Evangelists will listen to God's heart for the individual in front of them and they will listen for what he wants to say to them. A good example of this is when Jesus spoke to a woman caught in the act of adultery. Jesus' heart for her was for her to be free of sin; it was not to condemn her but to encourage her to stop sinning (John 8:6-11).

This was less about Jesus pointing to the morality of her lifestyle. Rather, out of love, Jesus was warning her of the consequences of her

---

[84] Examples of Jesus compassion to heal include Matthew 9:36-38 and Matthew 20:32-34.

sin. His intervention rescued her from certain death. Continuing with this kind of lifestyle would put her life at risk, if she got caught in the act of adultery again.

Evangelists are joyful and friendly people. Jesus is described as happy and joy-filled (Hebrews 1:8-9). Jesus was friendly, kind, gentle, and good to be around. Jesus was known as a 'friend of sinners' (Mathew 11:16-19). Evangelists will seek to be the same, emulating Jesus as the perfect role model. Joyful and friendly evangelism results from joyful and friendly evangelists (Luke 10:17).

Reaping

This strength brings people to a decision point in becoming a Christian. It leads people into salvation, incorporating repentance, new birth, water baptism and baptism in the Spirit, and helps ground them in their new life in Christ.

The evangelist represents Jesus' heart for those who are lost, that Jesus has come not to condemn the world but to save it (John 12:47). Evangelists show Jesus' redemptive love to people, so they can enter the kingdom, they should not condemn people. Evangelists have a passion to see Jesus get his inheritance: the nations and people of the world (Psalm 2:7-8).

An angel tells evangelist Philip to go to the desert road. When he arrives, the Holy Spirit then directs Philip to approach the chariot of an Ethiopian eunuch. The eunuch is reading from Isaiah 53, but does not understand about whom the prophecy is talking. Philip then explains the good news of Jesus and baptises him. Philip sees the salvation of the first Ethiopian, who was possibly the very first convert from the continent of Africa (Acts 8:26-40).

God often reveals to us the issues that are stopping people become Christians. Once Mark met two men drinking in the afternoon in a town centre. During the conversation they revealed how they struggled to believe in God because they both, at different times, held a loved one in their arms as they watched them die, feeling powerless to help. Through compassion, the evangelist draws such things out of people so they can bring God's redemptive love to their broken hearts.

Equipping

This strength creates an evangelistic culture in a church where all believers are equipped and confident. This strength aligns people's motivation with God's dream and his love for the world. It also helps people make the most of evangelistic moments.

Evangelists help to develop a supernatural lifestyle for every believer. They nurture, equip, mature, and activate all believers to be evangelistic by nature. The evangelist trains Christians to recognise evangelistic moments that God wants to invite them into as they are going about their daily lives.

The evangelist carries the answers to people's struggles with evangelism. They also have the ability to help people enjoy and seek out opportunities to do evangelism. Part of their equipping will be to help Christians find freedom in evangelism, so they can embrace the adventure it is meant to be.

Evangelists equip from the perspective that it is a privilege to partner with God in his dream to reconcile the world. They will not equip through guilt and frustration. If they do, it will create an environment where people are rarely honest about the struggles they have with evangelism and they are also unlikely to ask for help to overcome such struggles. In such an environment, evangelism will be more 'chore-ful' than joyful!

Slipstreaming

This strength creates an environment where people can freely and joyfully engage in evangelism. Whenever people are around this strength they get drawn into courageous evangelistic adventures where they find evangelism easy and enjoyable.

Courage is important in the Bible and is often involved in breakthrough. Jesus often told people to take courage (John 16:33). The evangelist carries courage and boldness for evangelistic breakthrough. They can share the courage they have with others, emboldening them in evangelism.

Evangelists can mobilise others to join in their evangelistic adventures. They do this by creating an evangelistic slipstream. A slipstream is defined[85] as 'an assisting force regarded as drawing something along behind something else'. When others join in their evangelistic adventures, evangelists draw them along with their strength.

Jesus often drew his disciples into what he was doing[86] and also sent them out to other places to speak about and demonstrate the kingdom (Luke 10:1-12). In this way Jesus created a slipstream for them, so they could do the works he was doing (John 14:12).

---

[85] en.oxforddictionaries.com/definition/slipstream
[86] Examples of Jesus drawing his disciples into what he was doing include Matthew 17:1-13, Mark 6:37 and Luke 22:7-13.

"Yes, you can pray for my back."

Mark was taking his usual drive to work. As he drove past a hitchhiker, Holy Spirit asked Mark to pick him up. Mark would not normally do this, but he recognised that Holy Spirit was initiating an evangelistic moment. Mark slowed down, pulled over and asked if the hitchhiker wanted a lift.

The remaining journey was forty-five minutes, so there was plenty of time for an opportunity. Mark built rapport with the hitchhiker, mainly sharing stories about their work. During the conversation he was listening to see if Holy Spirit wanted to speak to him about the hitchhiker.

During the journey, Holy Spirit told Mark that the hitchhiker had back pain. Mark shared this and it led to a conversation about faith and Jesus where Mark got to share his testimony of how he became a Christian. At the end of the journey, Mark offered to pray for the hitchhiker's healing, the hitchhiker agreed, and Mark had the opportunity to pray for him before he got out of the car.

Activation

Reflect on these verses:

> *So Christ himself gave the apostles, the prophets, the*
> *evangelists, the pastors and teachers, to equip his people for*
> *works of service, so that the body of Christ may be built up*
> *until we all reach unity in the faith and in the knowledge of*
> *the Son of God and become mature, attaining to the whole*
> *measure of the fullness of Christ.*
> Ephesians 4:11-13

Ask God:

- What do you love about me?
- Have you given me the evangelist gift? If so, what strengths do I have?
- How can I motivate and equip others to help them bring about your dream?

Pray:

> *Father, thank you for giving gifts of people to the church,*
> *including the evangelist. Thank you for designing the*
> *evangelist gift to equip me to be evangelistic and help me*
> *to thrive within evangelistic moments. Please help me grow*
> *evangelistically and introduce many people to you and your*
> *kingdom.*

To do:

- Write down what God said to you and meditate on it.
- If you know any evangelists, why not ask them to help you to become more evangelistic?

Further reading:

- Acts 8:4-40
- John 12:47-50
- John 20:19-23

CREATING SLIPSTREAMS

I have lived my life in the slipstream of experience.
(Elizabeth Jane Howard, Novelist)

"How you know?"

We were flying to Sydney via Singapore but had to unexpectedly stay over in Singapore due a problem with our flight. We booked a hotel, got a taxi, and headed down town. It was late when we arrived at the hotel, so we decided to sleep.

Mark and one of our children woke early and decided to get some food for breakfast. Where we were staying there were not any restaurants, so they decided to search for a supermarket or convenience store. Shopping for food in a foreign country with a different language and culture can sometimes be a challenge.

They picked up some food and headed towards the counter. As they were paying, Holy Spirit said to Mark in his thoughts that the supermarket assistant had pain under her arm and down the side of her body. After paying for the food, Mark asked the supermarket assistant if she had pain where Holy Spirit had said.

It became quickly apparent that English was not the supermarket assistant's first language, so Mark was not sure if the conversation would be particularly easy. Her initial reaction was that Mark was asking for pain killers, as she thought he was describing pain he had in his body.

Mark began to think how he could communicate to the supermarket assistant, knowing that she had misunderstood him. He decided to point at her saying that she was the one with pain. Mark was reluctant to point as it can be considered rude in some Asian cultures and he did not know whether it would be so in Singapore.

Mark decided that creating a moment for God to heal is more important than breaking a cultural norm. As Mark pointed at her, the supermarket assistant realised what Mark was saying and asked, "How you know?" Mark shared with the supermarket assistant how God cared for her and wanted to heal her. Mark then took her hand and prayed for the pain in her side to be healed. The supermarket assistant thanked Mark for praying and went back to her work.

Evangelistic slipstreams

In sport, 'slipstreaming' is important in cycling and is part of the tactics within sprint events. Wind resistance affects the speed of a cyclist and they can avoid this by using another rider's slipstream (also known as drafting). The rider at the front uses about a third more energy than those behind. Riders benefit most when they are closely tucked in behind the leader, which for professional cyclists is often as close as a few centimetres. More than the length of a bicycle and the benefit of slipstreaming disappears in road racing.

When Saul is anointed King, the prophet Samuel tells him that he will meet two men who will tell him that his lost donkeys have been found and that his father is worried about him. Samuel then instructs Saul to go to Gibeah to meet a procession of prophets, who will be prophesying. Samuel then tells Saul "The Spirit of the Lord will come powerfully upon you, and you will prophesy with them; and you will be changed into a different person." (1 Samuel 10:6).

In this story, Saul gets caught up in the prophets' slipstream, prophesying to such an extent that others call him a prophet (1 Samuel 10:11). This is a powerful experience for Saul because he was changed into a different person. Such slipstreams can significantly enlarge our supernatural experience of God.

A slipstream creates an environment where others can benefit from another's strength to the point where it rubs off and changes them. When people get in the slipstream of an evangelist, what the evangelist experiences, those in their slipstream experience too.

To put it another way, the evangelist introduces Christians to what being evangelistic looks like, so it can become a normal part of their life. This provides a very effective way of learning how to do evangelism. Being in such a slipstream can also change a Christian's heart towards evangelism, so it becomes enjoyable and an adventure they eagerly embrace.

The Evening Eastgate School of Spiritual Life[87] includes several all-day Saturday events within its programme, one of which is evangelism. On this day we both teach the students about God's dream, evangelistic freedom, and supernatural evangelism.

To help us do this, we gather many of our evangelist friends. Our aim is to have a ratio of one evangelist to three students. We do this to create an evangelistic slipstream that enables the students to enjoy evangelism and find it easier than they thought.

---

[87] eastgate.org.uk/essl/essl-online

At the end of the day, many students come back joyful, saying, "I never knew evangelism could be like that, it felt so natural and easy". Throughout the day they had seen miracles, heard Holy Spirit speak to them about unbelievers, and found courage for evangelism. The evangelists have not done the evangelism for them; rather they have created an environment where students are enabled to access the supernatural resources of heaven for evangelism.

"You can do all the talking today!"

The Daytime Eastgate School of Spiritual Life[88] curriculum includes evangelism. One method of evangelism that is taught is called Treasure Hunting. Students are asked to listen to Holy Spirit for clues and then go looking for people who match the clues. The clues include locations, appearance, names, and needs.

It was the beginning of the school year and a student Mark was paired with was Treasure Hunting for the first time. He asked her what he could do to make the evangelism a positive experience. She humorously said, "You can do all the talking today!" Mark smiled and replied, "You are too old for me to speak for you." (She was in her early twenties).

Mark initially modelled how it worked using his clues and then the student went looking for her clues. A few minutes later, the student spotted three people who matched her clues and she decided to approach them.

What happened next was remarkable. The student engaged with the group, shared her clues, led them to encounter God and prayed for them all. Mark barely got a chance to join in! She was benefitting

---

[88] eastgate.org.uk/essl/essl-dayschool

from an evangelist's slipstream. Evangelism is not difficult when evangelists create supernatural slipstreams.

Getting in the slipstream of the right covenant

In the Bible, the Old and New covenants have significant differences. The book of Hebrews chapters 7 to 10 compares the two covenants and is particularly helpful in this regard.

The Old Covenant was established between God and the people of Israel. It contained Ten Commandments and over six hundred laws. As people could not keep the Ten Commandments, a system of animal sacrifices was required to atone for their sin. The Old Covenant, amongst other things, reveals the holiness of God, the sinful nature of human beings and the need for a Redeemer.

The New Covenant is between God and Christians and is established through the life, death, resurrection, and ascension of Jesus. He is the sacrifice for all sin, once and for all, redeeming all who come to him, transforming them into new creations. The New Covenant, amongst other things, reveals the love and kindness of God and his desire for all people to be saved.

Paul compares the covenants in Galatians 3, characterising them as 'the law' and 'the spirit'. The Old Covenant brings law, judgement, and a continual sacrifice for sin. The New Covenant brings faith, adoption into God's family, grace and receiving Holy Spirit.

At the giving of the law, when Moses received the two tablets, the Israelites were sinning by worshiping the golden calf. This resulted in about 3000 people dying through judgement (Exodus 32:28). In contrast, at the giving of the Holy Spirit, about 3000 people were saved through grace (Acts 2:41).

Another difference is that in the Old Covenant the law forbids people to touch those who were unclean, such as lepers (Leviticus 5:2-3). Yet in the New Covenant, Jesus touched and healed lepers (Luke 5:12-16). The New Covenant brings forgiveness, healing, and restoration to people, whereas in the Old Covenant, those who were unclean were untouchable and outcasts. Within the Old Covenant people felt far from God. In the New Covenant, people are within reach of God, made possible by Jesus' death and resurrection.

So why do we discuss the different covenants within the context of evangelism? When we do evangelism we are representing the New Covenant, which brings love, acceptance, faith, repentance, new birth, forgiveness, cleansing, adoption, miracles, and eternal life. Any evangelistic message, conversation or prayer should embody the New Covenant.

If our sole evangelistic focus is on sin, separation from God, an angry God, and a distant God, then we may be in danger of representing the Old Covenant. If we don't get our focus right, we could potentially misrepresent God. When the disciples represented the Old Covenant, Jesus rebuked them.

After visiting an unwelcome Samaritan village, James and John suggested calling down fire to destroy them, just as Elijah did under the Old Covenant (2 Kings 1:10). Jesus says to them, "You do not know what manner of spirit you are of. For the Son of Man did not come to destroy men's lives but to save them." (Luke 9:55-56 NKJV).

Whilst sin and God's anger against sin is part of the gospel, it was not Jesus' main focus when speaking to unbelievers, because Jesus would save us from God's anger and punishment through his death on the cross (Romans 5:7-9). Jesus' good news of the kingdom realm focuses on the God of love, who is within reach, forgives sin, shows his kindness, and adopts us as his children.

Some evangelism methods focus on communicating to people that they are sinners in the hands of an angry God, which may echo the Old Covenant. Whereas Jesus forgave sin, healed the sick, raised the dead, cast out demons and said the kingdom realm is within reach. Jesus was called a friend of sinners, for eating with society's outcasts such tax collectors and prostitutes (Luke 7:34).

John the Baptist was an Old Covenant prophet, but with an important task of introducing the Messiah, and therefore providing a transition from the Old to the New Covenant. Whilst John was in prison, he sent some of his disciples to ask Jesus whether he was the Messiah.

Jesus replied, "Go back and report to John what you have seen and heard: the blind receive sight, the lame walk, those who have leprosy are cleansed, the deaf hear, the dead are raised, and the good news is proclaimed to the poor." (Luke 7:22). Jesus was saying to John: this is what the Messiah's work looks like. The New Covenant is different from the Old Covenant.

Earlier, when John pointed out to two of his disciples who Jesus was, they followed him (John 1:35-37). John's disciples were now disciples of Jesus, disciples of the New Covenant. Christians are children of the New Covenant and are followers of Jesus. Therefore, we will want to follow Jesus' approach to evangelism, representing the New Covenant.

What is within the evangelist's slipstream?

Within the slipstreams of an evangelist you will find seven key aspects. Firstly, love for the lost: God gave his son Jesus because he "so loved the world" (John 3:16). Being in the evangelist's slipstream connects people to God's heart of love, compassion, and mercy for those who are lost.

Secondly, courage and adventure: Peter and John were courageous despite being "ordinary men" (Acts 4:13). Being in the evangelist's slipstream gives people courage and helps them to overcome their fear.

Thirdly, freedom: Jesus set us free for freedom (Galatians 5:1), so we can be free in all areas of our lives including evangelism. Being in the evangelist's slipstream brings freedom from fear and freedom to be our evangelistic selves.

Fourthly, supernatural power: Jesus told us to heal the sick, raise the dead and drive out demons (Matthew 10:8). Being in the evangelist's slipstream releases supernatural power for the miraculous and for unbelievers to encounter the kingdom realm.

Fifthly, knowing Jesus is with us: when Jesus gave us the Great Commission, he promised to be with us always (Matthew 28:20). Being in the evangelist's slipstream brings an ability to partner with God in evangelism, without feeling alone.

Sixthly, joy: the seventy-two disciples returned from evangelism with joy (Luke 10:17) and there was joy in Samaria following evangelism (Acts 8:8). Being in the evangelist's slipstream creates joy, hope and strength for evangelism.

Seventhly, salvation: we live in a time where all who call on Jesus will be saved (Acts 2:21) and God's dream is to have an uncountable number of people before his throne (Rev 7:9). Being in the evangelist's slipstream brings people to Christ to become his disciples.

When we train people to be evangelistic, we want to create a slipstream whenever possible. We want to make evangelism and evangelistic moments to be fun, enjoyable, and memorable. The best way we have found to achieve this is to gather a team of evangelists for the training. A team multiplies what one individual can create, so the greater the slipstream, the greater the courage, compassion, miracles, salvation and joy!

As we equip other Christians, we find they start having stories of their own. God invites them into evangelistic moments, they hear Holy Spirit speak to them about unbelievers, those they pray for are miraculously healed and they lead people to Christ. It doesn't matter if they are extroverts, introverts, apostles, prophets, pastors, teachers, men, women, old or young, they all start to enjoy evangelism.

Treating people well

We have two passages of scripture that we regularly draw on to equip people to be evangelistic and do evangelism. Both these passages include great stories of evangelism and present similar models of how to partner with God in an evangelistic moment. One is Jesus himself showing us, the other is an ordinary disciple, but both show what is possible for us.

The first passage is from John 4, where Jesus is speaking with a

Samaritan woman. We have discussed Jesus' approach in this passage in a previous chapter but wanted to draw out some further thoughts from a training perspective.

Jesus wants a drink from a well, which was an everyday event. We can be invited by God into an evangelistic moment any time, any place, anywhere. We have God-initiated evangelistic moments with family, friends, work colleagues and strangers. God sees more possibilities than we do with our natural eyes. We may be standing next to someone who is on the verge of becoming a Christian and not know it!

Jesus' actions are counterculture in this story, because Jews didn't associate with Samaritans. When God invites us to partner with him, he may require us to break human traditions to bring the kingdom. This could include starting conversations with a stranger and speaking with people from different cultural or social strata[89]. It could also include those who are marginalised or living an immoral lifestyle, as this woman was.

An evangelistic opportunity may be seemingly out of our comfort zone, but if God is asking us to partner with him then he knows we can do what he asks. We can ask God for wisdom as to how we should approach the evangelistic moment, because we know he gives it generously (James 1:5).

There is a lot of interaction between Jesus and the Samaritan woman. The conversation between them is lively, full of questions, surprises, and revelation. It is better to have evangelistic conversations *with* people rather than preach *at* them. There are two people involved

---

[89] en.wikipedia.org/wiki/Social_stratification

in a conversation and so both people need to have opportunity to talk, ask questions, share what they think and be free to stop if they don't want to talk further.

When we are in an evangelistic moment, we may have a model in our mind about how it should go, but we may be speaking with someone who may have a different plan as to how the conversation should go. Allowing time for people's questions and points of view is crucial to the success of any evangelistic moment. If we don't take time to let them speak and listen to what they are saying, they are unlikely to feel loved and valued.

People are more important than any evangelistic model or method we may be using. We don't hound or chase people down when we do evangelism. We also don't argue or shout at them (Matthew 12:19-20). Leaving someone feeling loved and valued after an evangelistic conversation is important to his or her journey to becoming a Christian. It is important to treat people with kindness, dignity, gentleness, and respect (1 Peter 3:15).

Maya Angelou[90], the civil rights activist said, "I've learned that people will forget what you said, people will forget what you did, but people will never forget how you made them feel." If unbelievers are treated well, they are more likely to be receptive to the message of the gospel. Learning to build rapport with people is a key to an evangelistic moment being successful.

People will respond differently in evangelistic moments. Most will engage and show interest, but some will react negatively. Jesus loved the rich young ruler even though he rejected him (Mark 10:21). Regardless of how people respond to us, we will still want to show

---

[90] en.wikipedia.org/wiki/Maya_Angelou

them love. Jesus treated the Samaritan woman with respect and dignity despite her lifestyle.

In his conversation with the Samaritan woman, Jesus spoke about the kingdom realm, answered her questions, revealed her needs, and introduced himself as the Messiah. Jesus had a destination in mind for the conversation. After an initial conversation and after praying for someone, we can be ready to move on to the next moment, but God may not be finished.

During an evangelistic moment, we need to keep listening to Holy Spirit about what else he has in mind for the person. For example, the moment might start with hearing God speak to us about someone's need for healing, but Holy Spirit may also want to answer their questions, bring hope for a difficult situation, meet another need, deal with a misconception about God or Christianity, help a relative or friend, or they may be ready to become a Christian.

Learning to reach God's destination for an evangelistic moment is as important as learning to respond to the initial invitation from God to partner with him. To do this, we can ask Holy Spirit what he wants to communicate next to the individual in front of us. God may want to give us a revelation that will make them more open to the gospel.

Hearing God

The second passage is from Acts 9. This follows Saul's encounter with Jesus on the Damascus road. In Damascus there is a disciple called Ananias who has no knowledge of Paul's supernatural encounter with Jesus. God speaks to Ananias in a vision and tells him to go and pray for Saul. To make it easy, God gives him the address of the house where Saul is staying!

Even though God tells him that Saul is praying and has seen in a vision a man called Ananias praying for him to receive his sight, he is understandably reluctant because of Saul's persecution of Christians. God then shares Saul's destiny with Ananias: "This man is my chosen instrument to proclaim my name to the Gentiles and their kings and to the people of Israel" (Acts 9:15). This was enough for Ananias, who then goes to visit Saul. Ananias prays for him to see again and to be filled with the Holy Spirit, after which he baptises Saul.

This story does not tell us much about Ananias other than that he was a disciple. It does not say he was a church leader, someone who regularly saw miracles and healing, or someone who excelled at being evangelistic. It says he was a disciple, someone who followed Jesus. Stories like this can happen to any disciple who follows Jesus.

Hearing God's voice is normal to Ananias. We don't know if God interrupted Ananias in the middle of his day or whether Ananias was spending some dedicated time with God. In this conversation God gives Ananias specific instructions to go to Saul, who is in the process of becoming a Christian.

Do we expect to hear God like this? Our normal Christian experience can include God speaking to us during the day and giving us specific instructions for people around us who are near the kingdom (Mark 12:34). Learning to hear God in an evangelistic moment and responding to what you hear is important.

Some Christians can initially struggle to hear God for themselves, for other Christians and for unbelievers. They may not have an issue hearing for a fellow Christian, but they might do for an unbeliever. Building an expectancy that any Christian can hear God at any time for an unbeliever will help to overcome this issue. Practice will help too!

Ananias' reaction to what he was asked to do is understandable. Saul was persecuting and killing Christians! We may not initially want to respond to God's invitation to an evangelistic moment, for a variety of reasons. We can learn to recognise our feelings and process them. We can, as Ananias did, speak to God about what we think and let him speak further into what he wants us to do. Then be obedient.

In this passage, we see that God is already at work in Saul's life. He has already gone ahead of Ananias and done all the groundwork in preparation for Saul to get healed and saved. It's a set-up! Do you believe that God has set you up for success in any given moment when he prompts you to engage? Maybe with a stranger, to see someone healed and/or saved?

Getting the evangelistic moments 'right'

As we engage in evangelistic moments, some may not go as we anticipated, and at times we may feel we got it 'wrong'. Every evangelistic moment is an opportunity to grow and we should not let discouragement or disappointment stop us engaging in future moments.

Our definition of success is that you loved the person in front of you by being, doing, saying and demonstrating the good news of the kingdom. Regardless of what else happened, what went right or wrong, if you loved the person in front of you then you were a success. The more we see ourselves as a success, the more we will engage in evangelistic moments.

When Holy Spirit speaks to us about an unbeliever in our environment, we may not fully understand it or may even misinterpret it (1 Corinthians 13:9). People may also not admit at the time that what we share is right. We need to be prepared for these moments.

In such scenarios we often say we are "learning to hear from God and don't always get it right." We then offer to pray for the person anyway! When this happens, we treat this as an opportunity to keep learning rather than thinking we have 'failed.' Don't get stuck on one evangelistic moment that does not work out as you expected.

We are all learning to hear God and may not always get it right, but that is part of the learning process. Also, we may think we have not heard right, but some people only realise later that what we said was right. Some people receiving such words may also not tell you that what you say is correct because they may be a bit emotionally overcome or are not willing to be vulnerable with a stranger. If your heart motive is to do someone good and bless them, see them healed or pray for them, then there is no getting it 'wrong' or 'failure'.

Once when Fiona was in a supermarket, she thought she heard the word "eyes" when she was looking at the checkout person, so she asked the shop assistant whether she had a problem with her eyes. The shop assistant said her eyes were fine, but after pausing and thinking for a moment she said, "But, my neck and my back and my wrists, knees and my ankles are killing me. I have just been diagnosed with arthritis."

Even though there was nothing wrong with her eyes, Fiona was able to pray for her healing. Though Fiona heard the 'wrong' word, the evangelistic moment worked out. The lady was open to being prayed for and was touched on hearing that God loved her.

Mark was once having his haircut and he thought he heard the word "blood pressure." He asked the hairdresser if he had something wrong with his blood pressure. He said no and asked why. Mark then explained that he often hears God for people that he meets so that God can do them good.

After initially gently mocking him, the hairdresser asked Mark, "So tell me a story of when you got it right?" Mark was then able to share several miracles stories with him. Even though Mark heard the 'wrong' word, the evangelistic moment was successful because Mark was able to share many testimonies.

Getting practical

Jesus did not start the conversation with the Samaritan woman by introducing himself as the Messiah; he did that at the end of the conversation. Imagine how the conversation would have gone if he had started with that! In our experience in western culture, many people have unhelpful and negative stereotypes or past experiences when they hear the word God, Church, Christianity, Jesus, or the Bible (we refer to these as 'The High Five'!).

So, we tend not to mention any of these when starting a conversation, it helps to prevent the 'shutters coming down' and people ending a conversation before it has begun. This can be due to them anticipating being preached at, being told they are a 'sinner' or that they are going to hell. Saying such things will often repel people and cause them to disengage before you have an opportunity to put the kindness of God on display by blessing them, praying for peace, healing and so on.

People are more likely to engage if we first build rapport, create intrigue and engage in conversation before you mention any of 'The High Five'. Building rapport first will increase the level of trust in the conversation and it will be more likely that they will let you pray for a need they have.

When we are in an evangelistic moment, it can be helpful to think about how to describe the kingdom and introduce Jesus in a way that is culturally relevant to them. If Holy Spirit speaks to you about an unbeliever, discuss it with the person, asking what they think. Offer to pray for them and ask them to listen to Jesus themselves. Ask whether they felt anything when you prayed and if they heard Jesus speak to them. If they did, discuss their experience with them. For example, did they feel a sense of peace or feel heat in their body? Are they receiving a tangible experience of his presence?

Throughout any evangelistic moment, listen to Holy Spirit and ask questions such as:
- How do you see this person, what do you love about them?
- How do you want to show them your extraordinary kindness?
- Is there an event in their life that you want to talk to them about?
- Is there something you want to say to them or do for them?
- Do they have any questions that need answering?
- Have they had a spiritual experience or dream they do not understand?
- What aspect of my personal testimony would be helpful to them?

- Is there anything that is hindering them becoming a Christian?

From a practical perspective, respecting people's personal space, asking people if it is ok before you pray or touch them, praying with your eyes open, gently holding their hand when praying, not drawing attention to them when you pray all help make evangelistic moments successful (and so does good personal hygiene!).

"I hear noises in my attic."

Mark was looking forward to speaking at Alpha one evening on the topic 'How can I resist evil'. Before this, Mark had to do a return trip with work to Glasgow. The working day went well, and at the end of it he got into a taxi to go to the airport.

The taxi driver was very friendly and they quickly got into conversation. He asked Mark what he would be doing that evening and Mark said he was giving a talk at church about the occult. The taxi driver then talked openly about occult activity in his extended family and how it was adversely affecting his children at night.

He said, "I hear noises in my attic, it feels unusually cold and my children regularly have nightmares." Mark felt God's compassion for the taxi driver and felt encouraged that he was ready for such a conversation, due to preparing for the Alpha Talk. God had set him up for success!

Mark shared some of what the Bible says about the occult and how Jesus has overcome evil. He prayed for the taxi driver and his family to be free from the influence of the occult. He prayed that they would know God's presence and protection. As he got out of the taxi, he suggested to the taxi driver that he attend a local Alpha Course.

Activation

Reflect on this verse:

If any of you lacks wisdom, you should ask God, who gives generously to all without finding fault, and it will be given to you.
James 1:5

Ask God:

- Do my past experiences of evangelism hold me back from taking part in evangelistic moments?
- When I share the gospel does it represent the Old or New Covenant?
- Whose evangelistic slipstream could I benefit from?

Pray:

Father, thank you that I can thrive within evangelistic moments. I ask for your wisdom, teach me how to seek and save the lost. Help me grow evangelistically, learning from 'right' and 'wrong' moments. Help me renew my mind, so I can see evangelism as you do.

To do:

- Write down what God said to you and meditate on it.
- This week, why not get together with some of your Christian friends, and do some evangelism together?

Further reading:

- Galatians 3:5-22
- Acts 9:1-19
- 1 Peter 3:15

DEVELOPING LIFESTYLE

The world is my parish.
(John Wesley, Theologian and Evangelist)

"Faith keeps knocking on my door."

It was that time of year to arrange our annual boiler service. Mark booked an appointment online using a company we had not used before. The night before the appointment Mark had a dream whilst sleeping. In the dream Mark saw himself praying for the plumber for healing, having been told by God in the dream where the plumber had pain in his body. When Mark woke up, he knew this dream was from God! God loves to initiate evangelistic moments.

The plumber arrived and got on with servicing the boiler. Afterwards Mark engaged him in conversation to build rapport. After a few minutes Mark asked the plumber whether he had pain in his shoulders and across his back. The plumber said he did. Mark offered to pray for him, which he accepted. After a short prayer, the plumber was able to move his arms freely and without any pain, which he previously had been unable to do!

The plumber then exclaimed, "Faith keeps knocking on my door." Mark asked what he meant and he went on to tell Mark about a recent customer who, due to a lack of money, was unable to pay for the new parts required to repair her boiler. The plumber then reluctantly said to the customer he would have one more look to see if he could get it working, knowing he was unlikely to do so.

The plumber then said to the customer, "Let's try it one more time" and to his surprise the boiler began to work. He asked the customer, "Were you praying?" The customer said, "Yes, I was praying!" The plumber credited God, rather than himself, with the boiler repair! Mark asked if he had a Bible at home. The plumber said he did somewhere. Mark suggested he read it and find out what Jesus was like, because it is Jesus who is knocking on his door.

What would our nation look like if all believers were evangelistic?

At the time of writing the UK population is around 66 million. In a 2016 survey[91] 48% of people said that they believed in God or some kind of spiritual power. The survey also revealed that church attendance overall is in decline and is currently around 10% of the population.

We live in a country where nearly half of the population recognise some kind of spirituality, but most are not connecting their spirituality with Jesus. The other half of the nation does not believe in God or are unsure either way. Other religions account for only 5% of the population.

So how are we going to reach large numbers of people in the UK and other countries? Jesus and the apostles went from village to village to ensure more and more people heard the kingdom gospel. This was important to Jesus; he said to his disciples, "Let us go somewhere else – to the nearby villages – so that I can preach there also. That is why I have come." (Mark 1:38).

---

[91] faithsurvey.co.uk/uk-christianity.html

If every believer sees himself or herself as someone who is naturally evangelistic, empowered for supernatural evangelism and motivated to partner with God in his dream, then it is more than possible to reach large numbers of people. If every Christian is helped to overcome negative experiences of evangelism and is led into new supernatural evangelistic adventures, the good news of the kingdom realm can impact many more people.

David Jeremiah[92], author and pastor, said, "Evangelism was not a program in the Jerusalem church; it was a way of life. The believers' lives and behaviours created such favour with the population of Jerusalem that people were drawn to the Lord". Evangelism is meant to be a lifestyle.

Scholars believe Moses led over two million people out of Egypt. When the Israelites complained about only having manna to eat, Moses said to God, "I cannot carry all these people by myself; the burden is too heavy for me." (Numbers 11:14). In reply, God asked Moses to bring him seventy of Israel's elders so God could "take some of the power of the Spirit that is on you and put it on them." (Numbers 11:17).

When the Spirit came on the seventy, they began to prophesy. At this point, Joshua asked Moses to stop them, but he replied, "Are you jealous for my sake? I wish that all the Lord's people were prophets and that the Lord would put his Spirit on them!" (Numbers 11:29).

It is unusual in the Old Testament for the Holy Spirit to be poured out on a group of people, with the result being that they would all prophesy. When it happened, all of these people did not have

---

[92] en.wikipedia.org/wiki/David_Jeremiah

a problem prophesying. Even though they had not done it before, when the Holy Spirit came on them, they were able to prophesy.

Throughout the book of Acts, when people are baptised in the Holy Spirit, prophecy is often experienced (Acts 19:6). Paul, like Moses, also wants all people to eagerly desire the gift of prophecy (1 Corinthians 14:1). Prophecy is available to all Christians and Paul encourages us all to eagerly desire it.

When we are baptised in the Holy Spirit, we should not only expect people to prophesy, speak in tongues and praise God, we should also expect people to become supernaturally evangelistic. We suggest this should be the norm for every Spirit-filled believer. Holy Spirit is looking to wake Christians up to the joy of discovering how he has made them to be evangelistic.

Jesus describes baptism in the Holy Spirit as supernatural rivers of living water that flow from within us (John 7:37-39). Part of this supernatural flow from our God-given identity is being evangelistic. If Christians understand that being evangelistic is part of who they are, the more they will embrace it and expect it to be a normal and regular aspect of their daily life. Even if it feels to some Christians that being evangelistic is alien to who they are, that is not the truth.

This Holy Spirit 'river' flows out of us. It is something we are given. The river is not something we get into or out of; it is something we permanently have. This river flows out of us because we are the temple of the Holy Spirit (1 Corinthians 6:19). This evangelistic river brings fruitfulness and healing of the nations (Revelation 22:1-2). As we step into evangelistic moments, we find the supernatural life of God flows through us, like a river, to unbelievers.

Discipleship includes evangelism

Part of Jesus' discipleship was to send people out to do evangelism. As the number of disciples grew, the more he sent out to do evangelism and to proclaim the kingdom. He started first with the twelve, giving them power to drive out all demons and to cure diseases. They went from village to village to proclaim the good news of the kingdom. (Luke 9:1-6).

Later he sent out the seventy-two disciples in pairs ahead of him, to towns he was about to go to. Jesus instructed them to heal those who were ill and tell them that the kingdom of God had come near. He said to his disciples, "The harvest is plentiful, but the workers are few. Ask the Lord of the harvest, therefore, to send out workers into his harvest field." (Luke 10:2).

In both cases they went out equipped with power and authority. Jesus' instructions, also in both cases, were the same: depend on him to provide, stay where you are welcome, preach the kingdom realm and heal the sick. Whether we are part of an evangelism team or living our everyday lives, the instructions from Jesus are still the same.

When Philip went to Samaria and proclaimed the kingdom gospel it produced great joy in the city (Acts 8:8). The seventy-two disciples returned with joy and Jesus was full of joy through the Holy Spirit (Luke 10:21). Joy is a fruit of being evangelistic! When unbelievers encounter the kingdom realm, whether they feel his love, hear his voice, are healed, witness a miracle or are born again, we experience joy.

After the return of the seventy-two, Jesus said privately to them,

"Blessed are the eyes that see what you see. For I tell you that many prophets and kings wanted to see what you see but did not see it, and to hear what you hear but did not hear it." (Luke 10:23-24).

Jesus is saying the disciples are favoured to see people miraculously healed and demons cast out when doing evangelism. The days that many prophets and kings longed to see was the Holy Spirit being poured out on all people, which includes when Christians would bring the kingdom realm, heal the sick and be evangelistic.

We live in the time when God is bringing about the fulfilment of his dream to reconcile the world to himself. We live in this promised time, when the Holy Spirit is being poured out on all people and when everyone who calls on the name of the Lord will be saved. We live in significant times. God has designed and empowered us to bring in the harvest.

When we consider discipleship, what goal do we have in mind? We will want to see people grow in their love for Jesus. We will want them living in freedom and living in their God-given identity. We will want them to seek first his kingdom and his righteousness. We will want them to live their lives to please God. We will want to see them maturing and following their destiny. We will want them to have healthy relationships. We will also want them to learn how to fish for people (Matthew 4:19).

Making time to seek out and to give life to those who are lost

Jesus came to seek and save the lost (Luke 19:10). In the parable of the lost sheep, Jesus speaks about a shepherd who leaves ninety-nine sheep to seek out the one lost sheep. When he finds it, he joyfully brings it home and gathers his friends and neighbours to celebrate with him.

After sharing the parable, Jesus explains its meaning: "I tell you that in the same way there will be more rejoicing in heaven over one sinner who repents than over ninety-nine righteous people who do not need to repent." (Luke 15:7). In this parable Jesus reveals the heart of God is to go and search for lost sheep and to celebrate when they are found.

When Mark was in his teens and was in the early days of following Jesus, he lost his watch whilst out playing games with friends at dusk in an open field. He thought God would know where it was, so he prayed and looked across the field and saw his watch reflecting in the moonlight. How much more valuable are people than possessions? God's heart is to find and rescue people who are lost. We should never think it is difficult for him.

Jesus continues the theme of rescuing in his parable of the lost coin. The parable describes a woman who sweeps her house and carefully searches for a lost silver coin. After she finds it, she calls her friends and neighbours to rejoice with her over finding her lost coin. Jesus explains the meaning of the parable: "In the same way, I tell you, there is rejoicing in the presence of the angels of God over one sinner who repents." (Luke 15:10).

A silver coin has value and is worth searching for. Consider the lengths the woman in the parable goes to find the coin: she lights a lamp, sweeps the house, and carefully searches until she finds it. Have you ever lost your car keys in your house? Do you hunt high and low until you find them? We do this because driving is an important part of our lives and many of us cannot do without our car.

Western culture is often so very busy with many competing demands. Churches can be busy, offering engaging programmes for discipleship and community. Jesus took time to disciple his followers and to make time to be alone with them, because it was important to do so (Mark 6:31). Yet we also find Jesus made time to seek out those who were lost (Mark 1:38).

Corporate evangelism programmes can contribute to this, but Christians will have far more opportunities to be evangelistic in their everyday lives. Christians need time to intentionally search out individuals in their social, family, and work circles. In the parables about the lost lamb and coin, the shepherd, and the woman, all spent dedicated, purposeful time seeking for what was lost. Surely we should do the same?

When Jesus restored a demon-possessed man at Gerasenes, he said to him, "Go home to your own people and tell them how much the Lord has done for you, and how he has had mercy on you." (Mark 5:19). When he did tell others about what God had done for him, people were amazed.

It is important to take time to tell unbelievers what God has done for us, whether it relates to salvation, answered prayers, provision, or miraculous healing. We regularly share miracle stories with our friends, neighbours and work colleagues.

We find that the stories wake up hunger for God in people. The more we share the more people ask questions and show interest. You may think at times that people are not interested in God, so you don't speak. This is not kingdom 'logic'. Kingdom 'logic' is to talk about and demonstrate the goodness of God, then to expect interest and have an impact.

At a lunchtime team event, one of Mark's work colleagues said in front of his team, "Mark goes to a church that sees miracles, ask him about it." This led to an evangelistic conversation and follow-up later with one individual who had believers in her family and wanted to know more. People are often amazed at stories about what God has done in people's lives.

The DASEL Course

We created the course 'Developing a Supernatural Evangelistic Lifestyle' (DASEL) to equip Christians to partner with God to bring about his dream, and to enable them to bring the kingdom realm any time, any place, anywhere. The aim of the course is to activate believers into a lifestyle of supernatural evangelism.

The course helps people to discover how they have been uniquely designed to be evangelistic, get free to enjoy evangelism and start having adventurous evangelistic moments. The course is interactive and includes testimonies, teaching, group discussion, activations and learning how to put it into practice.

We run the course at our church, Eastgate[93] and at other churches in the UK and abroad. The course is run over several consecutive weeks or as a weekend conference. The course is divided into seven topics: Getting Motivated, Getting Free, Getting Evangelistic, Getting Supernatural, Getting Kingdom, Getting Culture and Getting Lifestyle.

---

[93] eastgate.org.uk

More information about the Developing a Supernatural Evangelistic Lifestyle course (DASEL) can be found at **www.godsdream.info.**

Mark T

The DASEL Course for me was an answer to prayer as I was at a point in my Christian walk where I felt so challenged to step out in faith and exercise the Great Commission. I desperately wanted to keep learning more about how I could grow in the area of evangelism and meet new friends who were on a similar journey.

The course for me was a chance to reflect on my motivation to share the good news and also start to look at areas where I felt afraid to do so. We looked at identity and how God sees us. We tackled lies that the enemy has spoken over us and I found this really freeing and the activations were really powerful.

I loved how even the shy people in the group started to become more and more confident in their gifting and really walking in love everywhere they went. Each week we heard more and more testimonies of love really being put into action.

For me now it's changed the way we as a family live and love. We are praying for people wherever we go and seeing miracles happen and people touched by God's love, and stereotypes broken of what they think a Christian actually looks like. This course is something the Church as a body needs – as the harvest is plentiful and the world needs everything Jesus offers.

Katrina

My husband Peter and I connected with the teaching on the DASEL course. Shortly after the course ended, we went away on a week's holiday. Whilst on holiday we explored the area using a 'hop on hop off' bus tour. Whilst on the buses we got talking with the bus drivers and were able to put into practice what we had learned.

We built rapport with each of the drivers and encouraged them. I heard Holy Spirit speak to me about each of the drivers. I shared with the drivers what God had said, telling them what God loved about them. On one occasion I spoke to a driver about how God saw that he was a blessing to his local community.

The bus drivers were responsive to what we said, and I was able to share the gospel with several of them. The DASEL course impacted and encouraged me to speak more freely about Jesus and his kingdom, knowing that God will bless people as I speak.

Developing an evangelistic mind-set

Getting people to see God's perspective on evangelism and think the same way he does about unbelievers is transformational. Establishing people in the Biblical truths and dealing with incorrect and unhelpful thinking helps to lead people to freedom and maturity.

To sustain an evangelistic lifestyle requires a mind-set that establishes a readiness, confidence, and expectation for God to regularly invite us into evangelistic moments any time, any place, anywhere. Knowing that God is committed to his dream and has done everything needed to bring about its success.

An evangelistic mind-set incorporates six key beliefs. Firstly, it is a privilege to partner with God. Being evangelistic is not a duty or obligation, it is our privilege. We expect to thrive in evangelistic moments, feeling his pleasure as we partner with him to bring about his dream of reconciling the world to himself (2 Corinthians 5:18-19).

Secondly, it is God's kindness that leads people to repentance (Romans 2:4). Therefore, in evangelistic moments, we put God's extraordinary kindness on display. We bring love, forgiveness, healing, provision, wisdom, encouragement, peace, light, mercy, and salvation. (Romans 14:17). His goodness knows no end.

Thirdly, Jesus is the good news and the king of the kingdom realm. Evangelism is not primarily about recruiting people to a church. First and foremost, it is about introducing people to Jesus so that they can be reconciled to the Father. Yes, we need to believe the gospel and declare Jesus is Lord to be saved (Romans 10:9), but it is primarily about putting our faith, trust and belief in the person of Jesus Christ.

Fourthly, all Christians share in Jesus' kingly mission (Luke 4:18-19). We are all anointed to proclaim the good news of the kingdom, demonstrating the nearness of the kingdom to people where we go. We have all been uniquely designed to be evangelistic. Evangelism is inherently supernatural, and miracles will accompany those who believe (Mark 16:17).

Fifthly, the harvest is plentiful (Luke 10:2). We expect people to become Christians during some of our evangelistic moments (2 Corinthians 6:2). The giving of the Holy Spirit at Pentecost fulfils Joel's prophecy and ushers in a time where everyone who calls on Jesus name will be saved (Acts 2:21). People are not far from God and experiencing the kingdom brings them nearer to God (Matthew 3:2).

Sixthly, the gospel is for everyone (2 Peter 3:9). We do not limit whom God may invite us to speak to in an evangelistic moment. Potential barriers such as culture, gender, class, sexual orientation, spirituality, poverty, sickness, and inequality do not have to hinder the gospel. We scatter our gospel seed widely (Luke 8:4-15) and shine our light wherever there is darkness (Matthew 5:14).

Developing an evangelistic mind-set and lifestyle will usually take time. It's a process that rarely happens overnight. Psychological research suggests that developing a new habit takes many months. There will be times where you get it right and times where it won't work out as expected. It is important to create momentum and to keep going, until an evangelistic lifestyle becomes your new norm.

The journey is easier if you commit yourself to incremental improvements, without putting any undue pressure on yourself to get there quickly. Doing the same journey with others brings encouragement and helps us to spur each other on. It can also help to keep a record of your evangelistic stories and celebrate what God does within evangelistic moments he invites you into.

Knowing God's pleasure as you embrace this journey is the best motivation. Enjoying the father-child bonding moments as he shares his heart for unbelievers with you is a privilege. Seeing unbelievers miraculously healed, encountering God's goodness, and choosing Jesus is the greatest joy. Remember that people getting saved initiates heaven throwing a party! (Luke 15:10).

"It's me that suffers from migraines."

Whilst on a family holiday we were enjoying a heatwave in Western France. We were exploring the market stalls around the harbour and our children spotted churros! As we queued, Holy Spirit spoke to Mark about a person on the market stall having migraine headaches.

As Fiona speaks some French, she shared what Mark had heard from God with the stall owner. The stall owner said she did not suffer from headaches, but the woman next to her baking the churros said, "It's me who suffers from migraines." The woman accepted the offer for prayer, and Fiona prayed in French that she would be healed.

In that moment, evangelism was not at the forefront of our minds, as we were enjoying time together as a family. Even so, we were able to recognise God's invitation to partner with him to bring the kingdom realm to people around us.

It was a privilege for us to take a moment to do this. Our children are now used to these moments occurring! Stopping what we are doing when God asks is not an inconvenience; rather it is a privilege to partner with him to bring about his dream to reconcile the world to himself.

Activation

Reflect on these verses:

> *Jesus replied, 'Let us go somewhere else – to the nearby villages – so that I can preach there also. That is why I have come.' So he travelled throughout Galilee, preaching in their synagogues and driving out demons.*
>
> Mark 1:38-39

Ask God:

- Do I see your mission to seek and save the lost as my mission?
- How can the 'river of living water' flow in and through me any time, any place, anywhere?
- How can I realistically give more time to seek out and save those who are lost?

Pray:

> *Father, thank you for seeking me out when I was lost. Thank you that your heart is to redeem and rescue lost people. I pray that I would know your shepherd heart. Help me to make time to seek and out and save the lost. Please establish an evangelistic mind-set within me.*

To do:

- Write down what God said to you and meditate on it.
- This week, whilst you are with someone who is not a Christian, ask God for something specific about them so that they will know that God knows and loves them.

Further reading:

- John 7:37-39
- Luke 10:1-23
- Luke 15:1-32

YOUR INVITATION

Live out of your imagination, not your history.
(Stephen Covey, Author and Businessman)

"Yes, I do have pain in my wrists."

It was a Saturday and as we needed some new plants for the garden, we decided to have lunch at a café within a local garden centre. After lunch, we picked up a few items for the garden and headed towards the cashier. As we walked towards them God invited us into an evangelistic moment. We both felt his love and compassion for the cashier.

Holy Spirit told Mark in his thoughts that she had pain in her wrists. After paying for the goods and building rapport with the cashier, Mark asked if she had pain in her wrists and she replied, "Yes, I do have pain in my wrists." Mark explained that God had spoken to him about her pain because he cared for her and did not want her to be in pain.

We asked if we could pray for her and she agreed. We prayed for healing and affirmed God's love for her. The cashier then shared that her hip also needed prayer. Fiona prayed for her hip to be healed. We encouraged her to seek God as he is near and left her encouraged and smiling. We can bring the kingdom realm any time, any place, anywhere.

The reluctant warrior

Gideon was reluctant to believe he was a mighty warrior (Judges 6:12). His reaction to being called this by an angel of the Lord was to point out that no miracles were occurring, and that God had abandoned Israel to the Midianites. God had a different perspective. The angel then told Gideon to go in the strength he had and save Israel (Judges 6:14), after which Gideon shared his low opinion of himself as being the least in his family. Similarly, Christians do not always realise they have evangelistic strength within them.

After this Gideon asks for a supernatural sign to help him believe that it is really God speaking to him through an angel. After the sign, Gideon followed God's instructions to tear down the altar of Baal and build an altar to God, though he did it at night because he was afraid of his family and townspeople (Judges 6:27). Correspondingly, Christians do not always realise that God is willing to show them a sign that they have evangelistic strength and to help them to overcome their fear of evangelism.

The next day the townspeople were angry that Baal's altar had been replaced and sought to kill Gideon, but his father defended him. After that the Midianites and Amalekites joined forces to fight Israel. The Spirit of the Lord then came on Gideon and he blew a trumpet to raise an army (Judges 6:34). Even so he asked God for two more supernatural signs. Likewise, Christians do not always realise their baptism in the Spirit enables them to bring in the harvest.

God then takes Gideon on a journey to trust him to win the war, so that Israel would not rely on their own strength (Judges 7:2). This journey involved most of the army leaving and hearing the interpretation of an enemy soldier's dream. Through blowing trumpets, breaking jars, and shouting along with God's supernatural intervention, the battle was won (Judges 7:22). In the same way, Christians do not always realise that they can partner with God to supernaturally demonstrate the kingdom realm.

Gideon emboldened his army, imparting, strength and courage so they could chase down their fleeing enemies (Judges 7:25). Similarly, Christians do not always realise that evangelists can help them to overcome any hindrances they have with evangelism and to create a slipstream to help them be successful.

The Great Invitation

Martin Luther King, the American civil rights activist, had a dream where there was no racism in the United States. His famous landmark speech was delivered to over a quarter of a million civil rights supporters[94]. Following his speech, he was named Man of The Year by TIME magazine and became the youngest person to be awarded the Nobel Peace Prize.

Five years later Martin Luther King was assassinated whilst in pursuit of his dream. Over thirty years later, his speech was added to the United States National Recording Registry, which is a list of sound recordings that 'are culturally, historically or aesthetically important, and/or inform or reflect life in the United States'[95]. Martin Luther King's speech still impacts people today. His dream has yet to be fulfilled, but many are still captivated by his dream and are working to bring it about.

---

[94] en.wikipedia.org/wiki/I_Have_a_Dream
[95] www.loc.gov/programs/national-recording-preservation-board/recording-registry/nominate/

Jesus gave a famous 'speech' called the Great Commission, where he invited us to partner with him in his dream to reconcile the world to himself. The difference was that he gave his 'speech' after rising from the dead, having already willingly laid down his life to make it possible. Jesus was also about to ascend to heaven and empower his followers through the outpouring of the Holy Spirit.

God's invitation is for us to be captivated by his dream and to help bring it about. He is inviting us to be swept up in the excitement of being part of his dream. There is no bigger or greater dream to get involved with. There is no bigger or greater privilege. God's dream is not yet complete. There are many who have yet to encounter Jesus, his kingdom realm and be reconciled to him.

We live in a time where "everyone who calls on the name of the Lord will be saved." As Paul writes, "How, then, can they call on the one they have not believed in? And how can they believe in the one of whom they have not heard? And how can they hear without someone preaching to them? And how can anyone preach unless they are sent?" (Romans 10:14-15).

There is a need for evangelists to discover their ability to equip and to bring the answers to the struggles that so many Christians have with evangelism. Evangelists help Christians to develop evangelistic lifestyles and to discover the joy and adventure of how to partner with God during evangelistic moments.

When we see evangelism from God's perspective, it will be natural to want to partner with our Heavenly Father to fulfil his dream. We will want to do our part. We will be attentive and look forward to being invited into evangelistic moments. We will expect God to do amazing things in the lives of unbelievers around us. We will enjoy introducing unbelievers to Jesus and his transforming kingdom realm.

We no longer want to be limited by historic negative experiences of evangelism. We don't want our future to be dependent on our past. God has a story to tell about evangelism. A story that involves freedom, fun, joy, and father-child bonding evangelistic moments. We can be part of fulfilling God's dream and have our experience of evangelism changed.

It is time to reimagine evangelism and see it from God's perspective. It is time to imagine every Christian bringing the good news of the kingdom realm within their everyday daily life. It is time to imagine people becoming Christians every day. It is time to imagine evangelism as God originally designed it. It is time to imagine creating disciples of all nations and completing the Great Commission.

Do you want to accept the privilege of his great invitation? As his child, his desire is that you take part in the family business. He has evangelistic moments just for you, within which he wants you to feel his heart and through you, touch the lives of unbelievers. God wants you to discover his story about evangelism and for you to have your own evangelistic stories.

In recent years, the church is growing in her understanding of what Jesus said in reply to the disciples asking him how to pray: "Your kingdom come, your will be done, on earth as it is in heaven" (Matthew 6:10). Heaven is full of people who love and worship Jesus. What if it was on earth as it is in heaven in this regard?

It's time for every Christian to thrive in evangelism.

A prayer

Father,

Thank for saving me and adopting me into your family. Thank you for all that you have done in my life. Thank you for wanting to involve me in introducing people to you. Thank you for inviting me to take part in the fulfilment of your dream.

I accept your great invitation and ask you to free me from any struggles I have with evangelism. Help me to see evangelism as you see it. Teach me to hear your voice in evangelistic moments and give me the courage to respond. Help me to love people with your love and to see them as you see them.

Please empower me with your Spirit so that unbelievers will encounter you and your kingdom realm. Lead me into many evangelistic adventures and let them begin today.

In Jesus' name. Amen

Printed in Great Britain
by Amazon

16734182R00149